Y0-CAW-279

MARYSUE
RUCCI
BOOKS

I'VE TRIED BEING NICE

Essays

ANN LEARY

MARYSUE
RUCCI
BOOKS

New York London Toronto Sydney New Delhi

Marysue Rucci Books
An Imprint of Simon & Schuster, LLC
1230 Avenue of the Americas
New York, NY 10020

These stories are true. The names and descriptions of some people and dogs have been changed to protect their privacy.

"Needlers" from *Knitting Pearls: Writers Writing about Knitting,* anthology, reprinted by permission of Ann Hood, W. W. Norton

"The Deep Dark Me" reprinted by permission of *Lithub*

"Three-Drinks Short" from *Drinking Diaries* anthology, reprinted by permission of Seal Press

"Old Dog, New Tricks" reprinted by permission of *Real Simple*

"Love Means Nothing" from Modern Love, reprinted by permission of the *New York Times*

"Empty Nest" reprinted by permission of *Real Simple*

"Travel Travails" reprinted by permission of *The Best Women's Travel Writing, Volume 12*

First Marysue Rucci Books hardcover edition June 2024

Simon & Schuster: Celebrating 100 Years of Publishing in 2024

Manufactured in the United States of America

1 3 5 7 9 10 8 6 4 2

Library of Congress Cataloging-in-Publication Data has been applied for.

ISBN 978-1-9821-2034-4
ISBN 978-1-9821-2037-5 (ebook)

For Denis

CONTENTS

I'VE TRIED BEING NICE

As soon as I sent the manuscript of my first book to my agent, I plunged into a downward spiral of shame and regret. Why had I sent it? The writing was awful. What was I thinking? When my agent finished reading it, he sent me a letter mentioning the parts of the book he enjoyed and highlighting the areas that needed improvement. The main problem, according to him, wasn't the writing. It was the protagonist.

"I just wish the narrator were more likeable," he said.

"I know," I wrote back. "I do too. I've been working on that all my life, ha ha ha!" Because the thing is, my first book, *An Innocent, a Broad*, was a memoir; I was the narrator.

"I'd like to see the growth you experienced," he said. "It would help if the narrative followed a trajectory showing what you were like before, and how you came out on the other side of this experience a better person."

"But I think I came out of the experience worse," I wrote back.

The book was about the premature birth of our first son, Jack.

He was born in the wrong month, in the wrong country, on the wrong end of our economic "trajectory." The dead-broke end.

"I was lessened by the experience," I went on to say, "if anything. I came out of it a defeated, depressed, empty husk of a person."

People must not have known as much about PTSD or postpartum depression in those days, because he replied, "I think if you do some serious reflection, you'll be able to recall how you were changed for the better by it all, and that would be very rewarding for the reader."

My agent was somehow able to sell the manuscript, despite its narrator's shortcomings. Later, my editor seemed to grasp the way this experience might diminish a person, but she wanted me to compare the feeble, struggling character I'd depicted in the pages to the strong, self-sufficient person I must have been before the whole crazy, fish-out-of-water birth story took place.

She wrote, "If we've seen you be strong and in charge of your life in the past, we'll feel more sympathy when we see you shattered."

I thoroughly examined the pre-motherhood part of my life, searching for any examples of character, strength, or fortitude, and all I had to offer as an excuse for finding none was this: I was young. I was in my twenties—just a few years out of college. Had I been more mature, I'm sure I would have had more to offer as a protagonist.

And after that, I wrote novels, because in my case, it's easier to create a likeable protagonist than to be one.

The strangest thing about discovering that I'm not the most sympathetic character in my own life story is that for most of my life, I was an inveterate "people pleaser," often going overboard trying to be nice. It's not that I needed everybody to like me. I needed them to love me. And not just my family and friends—I was the least nice to them. After all, they already knew I wasn't perfect. I needed the love and approval of complete strangers.

My desperation to please others became even more of an issue when my husband, Denis, became famous. He's an actor, Denis. He's Denis Leary. He was on the series *Rescue Me* and oh, a bunch of movies, but we met in college when he was an open-mic guy in comedy clubs. Maybe you've seen the movie *The Ref*? *The Thomas Crown Affair*? (This is something I do when I'm asked about my husband. I offer up a bit of his résumé because sometimes people confuse him with other actors. Years ago, I was doing a live radio interview about a novel I had written. Toward the end, the interviewer asked what it was like having Dennis Miller mouthing off around the house all the time. I said that I imagined it would be a living hell. Then I said, of course, I could only venture a guess, as I've never met Dennis Miller. The poor radio host had just spent twenty minutes thinking he was interviewing Dennis Miller's wife. He began stammering his apologies when it became clear that he had no idea whose wife it was that he was interviewing, and I felt so sorry for him that I ended up repeatedly apologizing to him for not being Dennis Miller's wife. When I got home, I told Denis—my Denis, Denis Leary—about it. He insisted that I had met Dennis Miller, and I said that wasn't Dennis Miller, it was Jay Mohr, and Denis became very annoyed because I never know who anyone is.)

◇◇◇◇

When Denis first became "famous," our kids were babies, and I wasn't really paying attention to what was going on with him. Dealing with his fans wasn't an issue because I didn't know he had any fans. He was still doing stand-up and he was also doing this one-man show he wrote called "No Cure for Cancer," at the Actors' Playhouse in downtown Manhattan, and I remember that he got some very nice reviews, but I was yukking it up on the Upper West Side "Mommy and Me" circuit—tumbling and clapping and rolling on the floor of libraries and gyms with my toddlers. Then he was on MTV quite a bit, but I was trying to get our kids into preschool, and it seemed we were always at the pediatrician. One night, Denis and I were invited to our first Manhattan movie premiere. When we walked in front of a long line of photographers, they suddenly shouted, "DENIS! DENIS LEARY! OVER HERE!" and the world went white from the lights of their cameras. My first thought was that he'd committed a crime.

"What is it? What do they want?" I asked, clutching Denis's wrist. "How do they know your name?"

"I've told you again and again. I'm fucking famous," he grumbled. Then I remembered that he had mentioned it.

I still never really know how to interact with Denis's fans. Denis spends a lot of time in New York and Los Angeles. He meets and converses with people daily. I spend most of my time in the country, in a little town where people pretty much ignore us. So when I'm out with Denis in the city, or when we're traveling, I still get very excited when people recognize him. We'll be walking along a sidewalk in Manhattan and another couple will pass. The man will say something like, "Hey! Denis Leary!"

Denis nods and smiles and keeps walking along, but I turn and wave and smile at the guy and his girlfriend, which prompts one of them to say, "We loved *Rescue Me*!"

I then interrupt Denis to say, "Oh my God, honey, those people loved your show."

Denis turns and says, "Thanks," then he tries to continue, but I'm still shouting to the people: "Wow, thanks, guys! That's SO nice."

We are now half a block away from these strangers, but my obvious interest in maintaining a conversation will prompt one of them to shout, "MY SISTER-IN-LAW GREW UP IN WORCESTER!" Well, that's quite a coincidence—Denis grew up in Worcester. So, I tug on his sleeve and say, "Denis, Denis, Denis—their sister-in-law grew up in Worcester." He shoots me a look of extreme annoyance and hollers back, "GREAT!" and drags me off. It's weird. The people are speaking English, but I feel compelled to repeat everything they say to Denis, like a translator, and then I often answer the people for him as if he is unable to speak.

I could offer many examples of the confusion and sometimes even injuries that resulted from my attempts to be the nicest person everybody ever met, but here's just one. We were at the US Open women's tennis finals years ago. Somebody invited us to sit up in their very fancy corporate box and watch the match, and we brought our teenaged kids and had a great time. You take an elevator down from the boxes, and when the match is over, everybody crowds around these elevators and shoves their way in.

We were riding down, packed in like sardines. Denis was staring up at the floor numbers that were ticking away, and I was staring into the face of a woman whose toes were touching mine. She was with a guy who was grinning shyly at Denis.

The woman smiled and said, "We're big fans," and I did the whole "Babe, babe, these people are big fans of yours" thing.

Then the woman said, "You guys must have people saying stuff like this to you all the time," and I smiled and said, "Yes, we do," and for some reason, both the woman and her boyfriend suddenly frowned and looked away. This caused me to mentally rewind and replay her words, and I realized that she had said, "You guys must *hate* people saying stuff like this to you all the time," AND I HAD SMILED AND SAID, "YES, WE DO!"

The elevator doors opened, and the people started to stomp off into the crowded pavilion, but I chased them through the crowd, saying, "No, wait . . . excuse me . . . I thought you said . . . ," but they were not interested in anything I had to say at that point. When I returned to my family, the kids were dying of embarrassment. Jack kept saying, "Why were you so mean to those people?"

"I didn't understand them; I was just trying to be nice," I said.

Denis grumbled, "Listen, I've said it again and again. Leave. The people. Alone."

You hear the term "people pleaser" in twelve-step recovery rooms a lot. Being a people pleaser in the recovery, or any therapeutic world isn't a compliment—it's a character defect. I've dabbled in recovery and therapy for most of my adult life, yet I've spent too much of that time trying to make everybody love me.

But then I turned fifty. And then I turned fifty-one. And not long after that I stopped ovulating. If you're a man, don't be embarrassed, this is important for you to know. Ovaries rule women's minds, bodies, and souls. But mostly our minds. I first heard about this ovary-brain connection while touring Vassar College with our daughter, Devin, during her senior year of high school. As we wandered through one of the old dormitories, our guide explained why the hallways were so wide. A theory in the nineteenth century, when the building was constructed, was that educating women could make them sterile. Sitting and studying would somehow force too much blood to rush from their ovaries to their formerly barren little brains to help them try to process information. Extra-wide hallways were constructed so that the hoop-skirted women could exercise by walking and running past each other, up and down the corridors. It all had to do with forcing the blood back down to the ovaries where it belongs. Our group of prospective students and parents were amused by this story.

"That's so funny," I laughed, and then my laughing sort of petered out because I realized that the original Vassar designers were onto something. I'd had one ovary removed during a surgery several years prior to visiting Vassar, and since then I had been unable to (a) remember to buy paper towels, (b) watch videos of flash mobs in malls without crying, and (c) understand what was really at stake in Iran.

When I had both ovaries, you should have seen me. I was smart.

Though I wasn't *technically* a genius, I could hold my own in a conversation that had to do with topics other than dogs or sex. Now that was all I really knew anything about. It was obvious that ever since I'd lost one of my two ovaries, I was working with half a brain.

I visited the Vassar website when we arrived home because I wanted to find out more about this ovary-brain theory. I thought I could work it into the plot of a novel I was writing. Maybe my character would be half-lobotomized like me after she lost an ovary. I didn't find anything about it on the college website, but I did come across a list of some famous visitors to Vassar. One of these was the writer/philosopher William James, who, in 1896, gave the young women a lecture on "Psychology and Relaxation." He scolded the Vassar girls for "trying to wear a bright and interested expression all the time" instead of "the stolid expression and cold-fish eye of their European sisters."

Ah yes, the "cold-fish eye." I knew it well. I encountered it every time I stepped off an airplane onto foreign soil with my dopey old "bright and interested" expression.

I worked half-heartedly on trying to be more stolid and reserved, but a couple of years later my remaining ovary decided to call it quits, and it became effortless. That's when I learned why people call menopause "the change." I'd read and heard that when women go through this change, one of the positive effects is that they stop working so hard at being nice to everyone, but I had thought it would come on gradually. I didn't know that one day I'd be simpering an apology to a stranger who'd spilled their coffee on me, and the next day I'd march out of my house, cast a cold-fish eye upon all creation and think: *Fuck off.*

My change coincided with my first introduction to Doodle Lady. I never learned her name, but one of her dogs is a Labradoodle or a Goldendoodle, so I know her as Doodle Lady. We'd just moved from Connecticut to our present home in New York State. Our house is on a quiet dirt road where many people like to walk. One day, as I was pulling out of our driveway, I saw that two women were walking along the side of the road, having a nice chat. I was just about to drive past when I saw a little Jack Russell terrier and a Labradoodle come bounding off the small field on the far side of our house. I slammed on the brakes. We have three dogs, and one isn't very friendly. Eddie is a rescue who came to us with some issues. He's not great with strange dogs or strange anything. I've worked hard at training our dogs not to go out in the road, but if dogs come on our property, Eddie will try to fight them or chase them off, and all my training will be undone. So, I stopped the car and rolled down the window.

"HI!" I said with a big smile when the women reached my car. I really didn't know who my neighbors were yet; I wanted to make a good impression.

"Hello!" Doodle Lady replied. "Beautiful day!"

"Isn't it?" I said, then, still smiling: "Are those your dogs?" The dogs were running down the road away from her.

"Yup!"

"They're so cute, I love Jacks," I said. (This is true—I'm crazy about Jack Russells). Then I said: "That's our field, there, where they were just running."

"Oh," she said. "It's lovely."

"Thank you so much. You know, it would be better if you didn't allow the dogs in there. We have dogs who aren't friendly with others . . . they're rescues and—"

"Oh, don't worry, my dogs get along great with other dogs."

I continued to smile and said nothing for a moment because profound stupidity can be difficult to deal with. Before Eddie, I'd never had a reactive, fearful, sometimes aggressive dog, but now I do, and I can't tell you how many numbskulls I've come across who somehow don't believe in the concept of anxious, fear-aggressive dogs. I've had people try to pet Eddie, and when I say, "No, please don't touch him, he's afraid and might bite," they become seized with the urge to press their hands and faces as close to my poor dog as possible. I've had too many people say, "Don't worry, dogs love me," while trying to grope the trembling dog hiding behind my legs.

But I didn't say, "Do you know nothing about dogs? Have you never heard of territorial behavior? Leash your dogs when walking by my house; I don't want them in there." Instead, I chirped something like, "Oh, they're so cute, I can tell they have great dispositions. It would just be safer if they stayed outside the fence."

She gushed, "You're so sweet, but seriously, my dogs love everybody!"

Then she and her friend waved goodbye, and power walked on down the road, her dogs of everlasting love bounding over hedges and in and out of my neighbors' gardens.

I was slightly annoyed at myself for not being more direct, but that year everything I'd understood about human civility and manners had been challenged. Presidential candidates made fun of one another's penises during a debate. Nasty trolls were all over Facebook and Twitter. Though my weird, off-kilter hormones ached to get me into every hateful fracas, I still wanted to "go high" whenever possible.

The next time I saw Doodle Lady, it was after a winter storm and half the field was covered with ice. Doodle and Jack were trotting across it like they owned the place. Eddie, our problem dog, doesn't just have what dog behaviorists call fear-aggression. As a special added bonus, he was born with bilateral congenital elbow dysplasia. Eight thousand dollars in surgery bills and three months of rehab later, he was not supposed to run on slippery surfaces. I had been out next to the field with him just a few moments before; it was sheer luck that we weren't out when the loose dogs trotted through. This time, when I rolled down the window, I wasn't quite as friendly.

"Hi," I said. "I was just outside with my dogs. It would be better if you'd keep your guys off our field."

This time she said, "But they weren't on your field."

This was a blatant lie. I lost my smile and just looked at her and then dropped my gaze to the leashes that hung from her hand. I was pretty sure she got the message, so I drove off.

I saw her a few times after that. Once, I pulled out of the driveway and she was walking up the road again. Doodle and Jack were running down my neighbor's driveway and were heading for my field.

I stopped. I watched her as she called them back to her. She removed the leashes that had been looped around her shoulder, but instead of attaching them to the dogs, she just sort of dangled them. She was going to wait until I drove past, but I held my ground. She was passing my window holding the Doodle's collar, and I opened it a crack.

"Oh HI!" she said, smiling.

"HI!" I smiled back, then I said, "There's a leash law in this town." But I said it sort of under my breath and I don't think she heard me.

The next time I saw her, Doodle was nowhere to be seen, but Jack was running down from the field. I slammed on the brakes about twenty feet in front of Doodle Lady and took my cell phone from my purse. I lifted it up so she could see it. She fingered the leashes that dangled from her shoulder. We were at a draw. It was a passive-aggressive showdown.

"I'll do it," I told her with my cold-fish gaze. "I'll call the dog officer if you don't leash them."

And her casual swinging of the leash said, "You wouldn't dare."

And my icy glare said, "Go ahead, make my day."

And then she made the dogs come to her and waved gaily, and I smiled and waved back and drove off.

But she knew. She knew.

Or so I thought, but the very next day, I was in my kitchen writing, when our dogs went berserk. I thought it was the UPS guy. When I looked out the window, I saw Doodle and Jack bounding down our driveway. I could see their paw prints in the snow.

That did it. I was going to . . . to . . . say something to Doodle

Lady. Yes, I was finally going to let her have it. But I needed to catch up to her first. She and her friends are power walkers, I couldn't chase them on foot; I'd never catch them. Plus, I was still in my pajamas. So I threw on a coat, got in my car, and drove right up behind Doodle Lady and her friend. Then I passed them because I had no idea what to say or do. As I reached the end of the road it hit me: I'm not just a "people pleaser" because I want to be liked; and I'm not just one who chooses to take the high road to protest the current nasty cultural and political climate.

I'm a coward. I'm terrified of making people angry. I have been all my life.

I turned the car around. As I drove back toward them, I saw Doodle Lady stop walking and call frantically to her dogs. I realized that this circling back and approaching them head-on looked like some kind of strategy on my part. Doodle Lady knew my car. She had seen me pass, then slowly turn around. That's sort of scary. When I reached them, I stopped the car, rolled down my window, and smiled, as I had so many other times. She smiled back. Then I said, in case she mistook me for all the other women who drive around in pajamas, "Hi, I live up the road. You know, the place with the unfriendly dog."

"Yes!" She beamed. "Hello there!"

"Look," I said, "I've tried being nice . . ."

And I stopped smiling. I just wanted to let those words hang in the air for a minute because I was quite impressed that they'd come from my lips. Doodle Lady removed the leashes from around her neck and reached for the Doodle's collar. Her hand was trembling. It turns out that saying "I've tried being nice" is like the cocking of a pistol or the snorting of a bull. It's not really a challenge—more of a warning. It's like the phrase, "No offense but . . ." It causes one on the receiving end to brace oneself because what follows is going to hurt.

At that moment I was Walter White from *Breaking Bad*; I was Sir from *To Sir, with Love*; I was young Jane Eyre. Why do we love those characters so much? Because they tried being nice. Then they stopped.

"I don't want to see your dogs on my property ever again," I growled.

"Okay, I'm really, really sorry, but I don't think they were on your property." See, she's only in her forties, Doodle Lady. She still thinks she must be nice to everybody.

"My dogs almost went through the window when your dogs were in our driveway a few minutes ago. We have rescues, one isn't friendly . . ."

"I know, that's why I always call them to come back to the road."

"And if he attacks your dogs, or you, you could be harmed, and my dog might have to be destroyed because you were so fucking careless that you provoked an attack . . ."

This is what happens when people pleasers stop pleasing. It's not okay.

"I get it," she said. "Trust me, the last place I want my dogs to be is on your property."

"So. Put. Them. On. Their. Leashes," I said. And then I said the words that catapulted me from my prime to my golden years: "AND STAY OFF MY PROPERTY!"

STATES OF MIND

Why am I like this?

Who hasn't asked this of oneself at some point or another? My mother, that's who. She doesn't believe in navel-gazing, and she's right not to—it's usually a stupid waste of time. Most members of my family of origin haven't tried therapy, we're more of a cocktail people, but before I was of an age where I found the apparent solution to my problems (cocktails), my frazzled mother presented the following conundrum to us, her children, on a regular basis: Why can't you be like normal kids?

To be honest, I think she mostly asked this of me, because I went through a rough patch that started around age six and ended when I found marijuana and alcohol in high school. Before I began self-medicating, I was somehow both chronically lazy and hyperactive. By the time I entered college, I was an alcoholic. Soon after college, I stopped drinking and entered the world of treatment and recovery, and I've spent the subsequent decades in and out of therapy, plumbing my navel to dangerous depths.

I've been fortunate to have found excellent therapy, but if I see an online quiz called "What Kind of Friend Am I?" or "Am I a Psychopath?" I take it. I always think this new quiz will unearth something those clinicians with PhDs overlooked. A few years ago, I came upon a quiz that promised to reveal where I lie on something called the "Self-Monitoring Scale." I ticked off the answers and realized that the quiz was about how well one gets along with others.

A statement like: *Even if I'm not enjoying myself, I often pretend to be having a good time,* was simple for me to respond with "always." Because I'm not a psychopath.

Or: *I find it hard to imitate the behavior of other people.* Another easy one—not me. I'm very good at imitating others' funny quirks, but don't worry, I'd never mimic you to your face. That wouldn't be nice.

And: *If a situation calls for it, I can be friendly, even if I really dislike a person.* Yes indeed. I tend to be especially friendly in that situation.

I thought I was being tested on whether I'm a conscientious and considerate person. A nice person. When the results revealed that I'm a higher self-monitor than 90 percent of the test's sample population, my self-esteem soared. Then I read that being a high self-monitor is a sign of low self-esteem. And the test wasn't about being nice after all. It was about trying too hard to fit in by seeming nice.

I do try to fit in. In my defense, we moved a lot during my childhood. My siblings and I switched schools every few years until I was fourteen. That was the year we moved from Racine, Wisconsin, to Marblehead, Massachusetts. Younger people, or those who have lived their entire lives in one area, might have a hard time appreciating how different the various regions of our country were prior to cable television and the internet. People listened to local radio and watched local television in the mid-1970s. We in the Midwest tended to dress like our peers but didn't know our hair and clothing styles were about two years behind our peer group's counterparts on the coasts.

And parenting was different in those days. Now, I think parents usually accompany their children when it's time to enroll in a new school after a move to a new town. It was late October when Dad dropped my brother, Paul, and me off at the curb on our first day at Marblehead Junior High School. I was in eighth grade, Paul in ninth. Dad gave us a wave and drove off. He didn't know what time school started, so we were late. The halls were vacant when we entered, but we could sense our bullies stirring like caged lions behind every door. We were new kids again, and this school's fine young sadists (according to the internet, 8 percent of the general population have sadistic personality disorder and a larger number have sadistic traits) were in for a pleasant surprise that day. I can still hear our footsteps echoing off the metal lockers and concrete floors; I can still smell the universal school aromas of that time—freshly xeroxed paper, glue, Lysol, body odor, stale cigarette smoke from the teacher's lounge, Irish Spring soap, and Love's Baby Soft cologne. I was shivering and sweating at the same time. Paul was stoic and silent. We found the guidance counselor's office, and then were each escorted to the homerooms we'd been assigned.

When I shuffled into my homeroom bearing the guidance counselor's note, the teacher stopped what he had been saying so that he could read the note aloud to the class:

Ann is a new student who has been assigned to your homeroom. Please ask one of the students to show her to the next class on her schedule.

If I were in a comedy club, my entrance to eighth-grade homeroom would have been something Andy Kaufman would have come up with—I was the kind of comedian you start laughing at before they even open their mouths, due to my dated clothes and hair. When I did finally speak—a Midwestern-twanged reply to a question from the teacher—it was comedy gold.

I gazed out at my audience of laughing eighth graders and let the shame wash over me. I was used to this—a new class, a new clan assessing an odd interloper, but here, there was more open mockery than I'd experienced in previous moves. Marblehead is a small town, and many of the kids had lived there since they were born, as had their parents, grandparents, etc. Salem, where nineteen people were hanged as witches in the 1690s, is the next town over. The region is still teeming with the self-proclaimed kin of those martyrs, but I've never met a single person who claimed to be related to the others—the finger-pointers, jurists, or hangmen. I think a few members of my eighth-grade homeroom would have been more likely to find people named Goody Hatecrime or Reverend Slutshame in their family trees than the accused witches, but I'm no genealogist.

Genealogist or not, it was obvious that some of my classmates were either closely or distantly related. There were exceptions, of course, but for the most part, they looked like one another, they smelled like one another, and they sounded like one another. They were preppy. They wore Lacoste shirts and Adidas sneakers. My school in Racine had been more culturally diverse—but a school on a remote Scottish island would have been more diverse than Marblehead Junior High School back then. I was wearing high-waisted, striped polyester pants, a polyester blouse, and platform shoes on that first day of school. In Racine, those clothes were still in style. They were sort of cool. In Marblehead, it looked like I'd hopped on *Soul Train* two years prior and forgot to get off at my stop.

The other students laughed helplessly whenever I opened my mouth. Not only was my accent wrong; it was almost like I spoke a different language. I learned that my dungarees were called jeans. A sparkling beverage that I had previously called "pop" (pronounced *pahp*) was called "tonic" here. Not soda—Coke, Tab, 7Up—they were all called "tonic" in Massachusetts back then. Milkshakes were "frappes." The water fountains in the halls were called "bubblahs." I never acquired a New England accent, but there were certain words that I unwittingly spoke with the accent because I had never seen them written—water bubbler was one of these, and as a result, I went to college still calling water fountains "bubblahs." Kids are adaptable, and it was only a matter of days before I'd persuaded my mom to buy me my first Fair Isle sweater and pastel-hued corduroys, and I was saying stuff like "wicked good" and "the balls" like everybody else—like the new "normal" kids.

◇◇◇◇

My brother, Paul, has always had a scientific mind; for Christmas, when we were kids, he asked for chemistry sets, model space rockets, and, one year, an ant farm. I was intrigued by his ant farm. It was a little universe sandwiched between two panes of glass, about the size of an eight-by-ten photo frame, and was filled almost to the top with sand. Paul added ants, which I assume came with the kit, and they scrambled around for a while before zealously launching into their work. They formed little teams and began digging intricate tunnels, bridges, and anterooms in the sand.

I was into pets, so I singled out one ant and made him my own. The ants were pretty much identical to one another in looks and psychological makeup, but I convinced myself that I recognized my ant, "Flicka," and that he delighted in the gaze of my enormous eyeballs. I loved watching him and his comrades go about their business—burrowing, schlepping grains of sand and food from place to place. I don't recall a queen ant—they didn't seem to need one. They just quietly worked their little asses off, designing a civilization with no planning meetings, blueprints—no arguing about who should work with whom; what should go where. Each group focused on a separate tunnel. Sometimes the tunnels would run parallel to one another, sometimes quite close, but never too close, because that would make both tunnels collapse. Everybody knew what they were supposed to do, and they seemed to know what the others were doing.

The problem with an ant farm is that if you move it too

abruptly, the sand collapses all the tunnels and chambers, trapping the ants beneath the sand. Once the surviving ants dig their way up to the surface, they're back at square one. Their world, which had been so carefully designed, is now in chaos. The group they'd been working with has become scattered, and they're alone among an angry and suspicious swarm of strangers again. They skitter back and forth, touching the glass, the sand, the other ants, with their antennae, but they don't know who they're dealing with, so there are some skirmishes and it takes a while to regroup.

Every time our parents told us we were moving, we braced ourselves for something that felt as seismic as the shake-up of an ant farm must feel to the ants. The network of friends we'd so carefully built, the understanding of our environment, the ability to recognize boundaries, stay in our own lanes, not interfere with potentially unhinged bullies, was gone. We had to start constructing a safe social environment from scratch. Again. Each time we moved, the place we'd left seemed perfect in retrospect. I hadn't appreciated how nice the kids in Racine, Wisconsin, had been until we'd left. When we first moved to Racine, I'd compared my aloof new classmates with the sweet friends we'd left behind in Michigan. And so on.

But there are upsides to moving a lot. I've met other childhood nomads—either military brats or the offspring of a wandering, discontented parent, like me, and we agree that there were some benefits to the way we grew up. I knew at an early age that people everywhere are more alike than they are different. Every time we moved, I could immediately identify the most popular, the biggest jock, the geeks, the nice kids, the bullies, and the most bullied. And the funny thing was, each school seemed to think their most popular and most bullied were the only most popular and most bullied on earth. They had no idea they had doppelgangers at every school in the free world.

And I don't know if I would have become a writer if I had grown up in one place. Sometimes we moved during the summer, and we hadn't met any of the kids in the neighborhood, so I spent a lot of time in libraries; I read constantly. I only liked books about animals when I was small; I believe the first chapter book I read, in second or third grade, was *Black Beauty* by Anna Sewell. I read it many times; it was my first experience of escaping to another world through a novel. If you haven't read *Black Beauty*, it was written in the nineteenth century and it's basically *David Copperfield* if David Copperfield were a horse—a very earnest, honest, beautiful horse, who, like David Copperfield, is thrust into one cruel situation after another, but never loses his kind heart and integrity. I devoured all the *Misty of Chincoteague* books, the Black Stallion books, *Lassie Come Home*, *Lad a Dog*, and then discovered books by Jack London and Rudyard Kipling. John Steinbeck's *The Red Pony* was my gateway to novels with human protagonists. And because I loved that story so much, I then read *The Grapes of Wrath* and most of Steinbeck's other books.

Why did we move so much? I'm no doctor, but my father has something that might be a combination of FOMO (he had it before fear of missing out was a thing) and a conviction that the grass is greener wherever he isn't. When he lived with us, he had a pattern of repeatedly finding a perfect new job in a new town and state. He'd get us kids whipped up into a lather of excitement by describing the many ways our future home in Utopia, USA, was superior to the grim wasteland we'd called home for the past year and a half. We'd pack up and move to the new town and there were months—sometimes even a year or two—when he seemed content. We'd finally found a place suitable enough for my father to call "home." Then some deep-rooted dissatisfaction would return; he'd attribute the source of his discontent to his lousy job or our lousy town, and he'd be on the prowl for a better job and a better place to live.

I googled "grass is always greener psychology" to find out if there's a clinical name for what my father has, and it turns out that's exactly what it's called: "the grass is greener syndrome." But according to the internet, this syndrome has more to do with people who have trouble committing to intimate relationships with other people. They meet an interesting new person and fantasize about how their life will be perfect with that person. If the person returns their love, there's a short honeymoon phase when everybody is happy. But soon, Mr. Grass Greener starts to see flaws in Ms. Perfect. She's gained a few pounds since they met; her laugh, which he once thought charming, is now like nails on a chalkboard. He would be so much happier if he could spend eternity with this amazing new person he's just met. This new person is perfect. My dad's need to change places seems to drive him more than his need to replace intimate partners, because he's in his eighties now and he's been married only three times, but he's moved every few years since I was born.

In the addiction/recovery world, people talk about trying "geographical cures." A "geographical" is when an active alcoholic or addict decides that the reason their life is miserable isn't because the whole town knows they're a drunk—it's because the town, and everyone in it, sucks. People in twelve-step meetings say things like, "I got fired, my girlfriend threw me out, so I decided to take a geographical." Often followed by: "But wherever I went—there I was." My father isn't an alcoholic or an addict, but he has always sought geographical cures for whatever ails him. I used to think it had to do with us. My parents married so young—my father was twenty-three, my mother twenty. My brother was born after a year, and I arrived the year after that. Maybe Dad was unhappy being strapped down with a family at such a young age—after all, wherever he went, there we were. But my parents divorced in the 1970s, and Dad moved many times after that without us.

He and his wife, Terry, now live in Florida. They've lived in several towns in Florida over the years. Each town was the best town in Florida when they moved there. Then the honeymoon was over—they were moving on from that hellhole. The new town was perfect for them.

My father says he never imagined retiring in Florida. He first retired to one part of Southern California, then another. Then he and Terry moved to a remote island near Seattle that required over a day of travel for any of his or her children who might want to visit them. They ended up in Florida because my father hates cold weather. Now he seeks constant affirmation that Florida is the best place on earth, so he seems glued to Fox News and the Weather Channel. Whenever there's a cold snap, Dad calls me and my siblings, unable to suppress his glee.

"Just saw the temperature up there. Ten degrees," he'll say on a January morning. "Man-oh-man, that's cooooold. We're thinking of you up there."

"Thanks!" I say, taking up my part in a pointless, decades-long passive-aggressive sparring match from which neither of us can surrender. All he wants is my envy, is that so much to ask? He just wants me to believe he's happier than me; why can't I indulge him in this? Instead, I say, "We're hoping the temperature will stay low enough for the ponds to freeze. Denis loves pond hockey. It's been too warm, but you know, we love winter."

"I just saw that it's below zero up in Vermont," Dad pivots. My sister, Meg, and her husband, Mark, live in Vermont.

"I know—they're in heaven; they're having a great ski season," I reply.

"I'd hate to be digging my car out of that much snow, I'll tell you that," Dad says. "Jeez, I felt sorry for them when I saw the weather report."

My sister is a better person than me. Or she's just busier and doesn't have time for verbal pillow fights that go on and on.

"Yeah, it sucks—it's been snowing for days," she says when our father calls to tell her how much better his weather is than hers. Meg, throwing her skis in the back of her car, tells him what he wants to hear. She pretends she's jealous, just so she can get off the phone and head to her favorite place—the ski slopes. "Eighty degrees? You're so lucky. If only we lived in Florida."

"You can! When you and Mark retire, you should move down here. But not here. We're moving to a town about twenty miles up the coast. This town is just too touristy. We're not crazy about the people. Not our type. But the place we're moving—it's perfect."

My dad should take the online quiz I took the other day. It's called "What U.S. State Are You?" Apparently, finding out which American state I most resembled would reveal what kind of person I am. I answered various questions about what kind of activities I enjoy, what I like to eat. Am I a beach or a mountain person? I'm neither a beach nor a mountain person, so I was very surprised to learn that I'm California.

"Your interests are vast and diverse, so what fits your dynamic personality better than the Golden State? You can surf it up at the beach in the morning, make it to the mountains by nightfall, and hit up Disneyland the next day if you feel inclined. As long as you're hugging the Pacific Coast, you're happy. Shine on!"

This was ridiculous—I'm no California. I don't surf. I hate Disneyland.

"Not the results you expected?" the quiz asked. It provided a link for me to see other results. I clicked on the link and was told that I might also be Texas.

No. No. No. I'm not Texas.

I clicked the link to other alternatives. The test moved me from Texas to Montana, Utah, and Arizona until I was told that I'm actually New York. I thought this must be the correct answer, because I live in New York. I love New York. But then I read why I was supposed to be New York:

"You are a city mouse, and proud! Fast-paced, career-oriented, and a bit of a thrill-seeker, you belong in the state whose major city never sleeps! And if you yearn for nature—take a train up the Hudson Valley and soak it in. You're the center of the universe, so start spreadin' the news . . ."

That really isn't me, I'm terrified of thrills, I need my sleep. I clicked for another result and moved from Maine to North Carolina, then to Idaho and Minnesota, but everywhere I went, there I wasn't.

COMING OF AGE

I remember the day I became a woman. I was fourteen and we'd recently moved to a modern house with a metal spiral staircase between the first and second floor. In addition to the color TV in our family room, we had a small portable black-and-white TV that my siblings and I fought over. One day, I snuck into my sister Meg's room, grabbed the TV set off her dresser while she was taking a shower, and raced from her room, but when I started down the stairs, I slipped and tumbled the rest of the way down. By the time I landed at the bottom, not only was the TV antennae broken, but I had also fractured two toes and begun menstruating. At the top of the stairs, I was still the only one of my friends who didn't have a period. At the top, I'd wanted to watch *The Beverly Hillbillies.* At the bottom, I was capable of bearing children. Within weeks, *General Hospital* was my new favorite show.

Quite a few lightning-quick decades later, I was at the checkout of our local grocery store. When the cashier scanned my final item, she said brightly, "And you're a senior?"

Because she seemed so excited, I said, "I think so, I just turned fifty-seven."

I had recently joined a senior tennis league that was for women fifty-five and older, which was exciting to me, because it happened to be a good team, so I now thought of myself as a young senior. But this woman's hand flew to her mouth, her cheeks turned crimson, and she whispered, "Oh no, I'm really sorry. That's not a senior."

"Okay," I said, still not fully understanding why she was so rattled.

"Seniors are sixty-five and older—they get a five percent discount," she said, helping me place my things into a grocery bag. "Five percent off is a lot, so, you know, I like to ask."

"Of course," I said.

Then she said: "I'm usually good when it comes to guessing people's ages."

Now that stung. I know she was trying to be nice, but she was doing something that I do sometimes—I over-apologize and in doing so, dig the unintended dagger in to its very hilt. Now I knew why she was mortified. She had just said that I look like I'm at least sixty-five, and I hadn't even been fifty-seven for a week. Had this been a college-age kid, I'd have thought nothing of it, but this cashier was as oldish as me. The worst part of it was, this wasn't one of those days that I threw on some sweats and left the house without glancing in the mirror. I was wearing makeup and concealer that was supposed to hide my wrinkles. I was wearing a trendy top that my daughter had left at the house and very cool sunglasses when this woman asked me if I was a senior citizen.

A few years prior to this, I'd been at another grocery store when a young cashier asked me for my ID because I was buying beer for a party.

"My ID! Well, yes, I most certainly do have my ID!" I said, giddily handing her my driver's license. "You're going to die when you see my birthday," I said, and I did a little humble braggy shrug for the benefit of the person behind me. The cashier said, barely glancing at my driver's license, "Yeah, we have to ask everyone who buys alcohol . . . state law." She pointed to an official notice taped to the cash register saying as much.

I had just moved to New York State from Connecticut, so I didn't know that asking old people for IDs was the law, but it didn't matter, I felt great. I went from there to our town's small liquor store, because, as I said, we were having this party. I bought some vodka, tequila, and wine. A man who appeared to be roughly my age rang me up and said, "Cash or credit?"

I handed him my credit card and driver's license, and when he just took the credit card, I said, "Don't you want to check my ID?"

"For what?" he asked, shooting me a suspicious look.

"I just got carded at the grocery store. Apparently, it's state law—you have to ask everybody who buys alcohol for their ID," I said, nudging mine closer to him.

He just stared at me.

"State law," I said with a meek smile.

"There's no law that says you have to ID people who are obviously older than twenty-one," he snapped.

There was nobody in the store but us. It's not like he had other things to do; the machine was processing my card, but he seemed annoyed that we were even having this conversation. I mean, what was this guy's deal? It felt like just a few years prior, I was trying to avoid getting carded at liquor stores because I was underage. I remember once using eyeshadow under my eyes to look sallow and old. Now, this man was willing to break the law just to make me fully understand how old I look (and am).

I said, in what used to be a workably flirty tone, "Well, I'll tell you what—it made me feel great being carded like that. Maybe you should start doing it. Why not ask everybody for their ID? I'd come back here every day if I thought you'd make me prove I'm at least twenty-one."

The machine rolled out my receipt and he silently pushed it and a pen at me.

"Seriously," I continued, as I signed the receipt. "I'd come and buy stuff here all the time if I thought you were going to card me! And the funny thing is"—I laughed here, a little too hard and a little too long—"I don't even drink."

"Do-you-have-an-ID-there-happy-now?" he said in a monotone while shoving the ID back at me.

"Yes," I said, no longer laughing. I opened my wallet and replaced my driver's license with great purpose. "I'm very happy. Thank you."

He was kind enough to carry the box of booze out to my car, and I thanked him, but I still couldn't let this go.

"Come on," I said, "it's a good idea, admit it." I used to be able to jolly-up people like this, I used to have some kind of flirt game when it came to grouches, but as he turned back to the store, he said, "Yeah, I'll put that one on my vision board."

My early fifties were transformational years for me. Photos of middle-aged supermodels with dazzling manes of silvery hair duped me into "growing out my gray." Our hair goes gray early in my family; I found my first gray hair in my late twenties. My daughter insists she found hers when she was twelve. I was tired of having that silvery stripe appear along my part every six weeks and found lots of advice on the internet about how to grow out the old color-processed hair without looking like a skunk. The secret involved hats, for the most part. It took about two years until I had the final haircut that removed the last inches of dyed, mousy-brown hair. Now I was a silver fox. According to me.

Once my hair was all gray, I didn't color it for two years and I thought I looked quite chic. We don't have the best lighting in our bathroom. But I had some evidence that backed up my self-assessment. When I was all gray, I had more men flirt with me—I'm talking about total strangers—than I'd had in my early twenties. I'd go out to our mailbox and a man jogging slowly by would circle back to say hello. He lived on the next street over, he told me—how strange we'd never met. Men at the gym grinned, and one even winked at me while I was on the treadmill; guys in supermarkets and the library found ridiculously obvious ploys to get my attention.

"I'll get that for you, sweetheart," a man said one day as I tried to reach a box of cereal on a high shelf in the supermarket. His cane cut through the air like a sword, and cereal boxes rained down upon us.

"Thank you," I said, scrambling to pick up the boxes while pretending not to notice that my gallant cereal knight's eyes were burning a hole on my ass.

"Raisin Bran, huh?" this player purred into my ear when I stood back up. "My favorite too, keeps me regular. You could set your watch by my bowels. Every morning, eight o'clock sharp. You live in the area?"

Oh, I forgot to mention that all the adoring male attention I received during my years as a silver fox was from men who were between eighty and a hundred years old.

Finally, I figured out what was going on. I had broken a bone in my hand and couldn't wear my wedding ring for a while. When I was able to wear it again, I couldn't find the ring for about a year. One day, I opened the glove compartment of our pickup truck and there it was. It turned out that these old men thought I was single and still had pretty good gams for a senior citizen.

My friend Martha said to me one day, "Why don't you color your hair?"

I told her that I was sick of coloring it and I always admired women with wonderful gray hair. "I think it's very attractive on certain women," I said.

"It is," Martha said. "I just don't think you're one of those women." Martha is the busiest person I've ever met, and she doesn't have time for bullshit, so she's very direct, and she also loves fixing things that aren't working. I wasn't convinced she was right, but soon after that, I was on my way to get a haircut, when my friend Anni called. I told her I was heading to a hair salon, and she asked, in far too delighted a tone, "Are you having your color done?"

I said that I wasn't. She was silent. Then I asked if she thought I should.

"I think so," she said. "I think gray hair makes you look older than you are, and who wants to look older?" I realized then that true friends tell you the truth. Anni and Martha were right. I've complimented many women on their beautiful silvery hair, and those women have told me they receive lots of compliments on their hair. Nobody ever told me they liked my old-looking white hair. My hair wasn't salt-and-pepper, it had no dramatic streaks of white and charcoal. It was just flat white. My amazing hairstylist had extra time that day and was thrilled to add some "lowlights" to my gray. Now I'm blondish again. I no longer wonder who the old lady is in group photos with my friends, and the guys with walkers just keep walking. I'm not the super-fit former suffragist that they used to think I was.

In addition to being prematurely gray, I became prematurely deaf in my early forties. I'm told by my doctor and my family that it started much earlier than that. Our daughter's first word was "What?" I guess I've always said it a lot, but it wasn't until I was in my forties that I finally realized there was a serious problem with my ears. At that time, I didn't think I had a hearing problem; I had a noise problem. I used to write in a tiny room in our attic. The heat and air-conditioning units were adjacent to that room, and they were noisy. One night, I couldn't stand the loud, constant whooshing sound that had plagued me all winter while I was holed up there finishing a novel. I turned off the heat; it was warm enough. I sat back down. I could still hear that whooshing fan. I checked the thermostat. The fan was off. I went downstairs. I still heard it. I heard it for the rest of that night and have heard it every second of every day since then. Like millions of people, I have tinnitus. Once I was aware of it, I was very aware of it.

A quick internet search revealed the devastating news that I had a brain tumor. I made an appointment with an ear, nose, and throat specialist and cycled through the stages of grief surprisingly fast, arriving at the acceptance stage in about a day. I focused on how lucky I've been, what a wonderful life I'd been blessed with. Yes, it had been a short life, but I wouldn't trade it for anybody's.

It turned out that I didn't have a tumor, I have something called otosclerosis. My doctor told me that my hearing test revealed severe hearing loss on one side, but only moderate loss in my "good" ear. Tinnitus often accompanies hearing loss—it has to do with how nature abhors a vacuum. If sound can't enter your ear, the body sometimes fills the void with, in my case, white noise. Very loud white noise.

Otosclerosis is genetic, my doctor explained. It's not terribly rare, but he told me that it was unusual to have it diagnosed at my age. He had just outlined my options, which included hearing aids and/or surgery, so I assumed he meant that most people get otosclerosis in their eighties. In fact, it's usually diagnosed in one's late twenties. He thought I probably hadn't noticed that my hearing had been slowly deteriorating for years.

Many things suddenly made sense.

Denis and I used to watch movies most nights. We had a very comfortable sofa. If I got tired and rested my head on a pillow on my left, I almost instantly fell asleep. When I sat on his other side and rested my head on a pillow to the right, I stayed awake. The reason why was because I had (and still have) almost no hearing in my right ear. That's the ear with the loudest tinnitus. I don't know why I didn't notice that I couldn't hear the movie when I put my good ear against a pillow. I just thought the movie was suddenly too confusing, so I dozed off.

Another clue happened one day in our local supermarket. This was when we'd lived in our small town in Connecticut for many years and I knew almost everybody who worked or shopped in that store. On that day, I had been listening to music in my car. It was a playlist from the 1980s—Talking Heads, B-52s, that kind of stuff. I parked my car and went into the store. Denis had texted me a grocery list. I was also becoming farsighted as most fortysomethings do, so I held my phone at arm's length in front of me to read his list, awkwardly steering the cart with my free hand. The crazy thing was that this hit song from the eighties—the exact same song I'd been listening to in my car—was faintly playing in the store. I wondered if I'd been listening to the radio in the car and perhaps the store's sound system was tuned to the same station. I said hello to a girl who'd been a classmate of my daughter's. She scowled in reply and scuttled sideways to let me pass. I waved or nodded greetings to others, and they all stared at me in the strangest way.

When you have one-sided hearing loss, sounds seem to come

from the opposite direction. I had thought the music was coming from speakers in the ceiling someplace. It turned out that the music was coming from my phone. It was very faint to me, but it was extremely loud to everybody else. I was pushing a cart through the store and staring at a phone that I held out in front of me; a phone that was blaring "Love Shack."

Now I finally have a set of hearing aids that work. I still need subtitles on TV, but I can hear birdsongs and the chorus of peepers in spring, rain on the roof, wind rustling through leaves on a summer day, and many beautiful sounds that I hadn't noticed were lost to me, until I could hear them again.

NEEDLERS

I like to think of myself as an open-minded, accepting person, but I do have some personal biases, and there's a certain group that I find insufferable.

I'm talking about the knitting community.

I have nothing against people who knit in private. It's really of no concern to me what adults choose to do in their own homes. And certainly, I have nothing against professional knitters; the world must be scarved. No, I mean the public knitters, the ones who want to shove it in your face all the time.

Full disclosure: I am unable to knit. I have the small-motor skills of a four-year-old. So I admit that it might be envy that fuels my hate, but there's something else, and I know I'm not alone. If the public knitter thought her behavior was pleasing to others, she wouldn't be so stealthy about it. She'd carry her handiwork and her tools around in the open. Instead, the knitter will wander into a room like any other person, carrying a normal-looking bag, usually a tote. If the tote is quilted or felted, or in any other way appears to be handmade, you're right to be suspicious. Don't rush to judgment solely based on this accessory. A dear aunt or a mother might have made the bag. In private. It could contain anything—magazines, books, or a snack. But keep in mind, this is how she works, the knitter. This is how she insinuates herself into polite society. When she sits down, this is the time to assess her carefully. Look for this tell: she will almost always take a moment, just after she settles herself into her chair, to smile thoughtfully at the air in front of her. If you are able to do so, leave now. Often, this is not possible, and you'll be forced to watch as she reaches into that seemingly benign satchel and extracts her instruments of torture—her yarn and needles and whatever she is currently knitting. Try as you might, you will be unable to avoid glancing at her handiwork, and when you do, you'll catch the knitter's satisfied little nod as she flattens the woven panel out on her lap and counts the stitches. The little nod is meant for you and everybody else in the room. "Yes," the little nod says, "I thought so. I am perfect."

Does my hatred seem petty and unwarranted? Here's another reveal: I fell in love with a knitter once, and perhaps herein lies the root of my intolerance. Perhaps I hold all knitters up to too high a standard. I compare them to her, and they always fall short. It happened when I was confined to a hospital bed in London. She and I were both young. Yes, my knitter was female, and I am heterosexual, but I was in a maternity ward in a foreign city, surrounded by women. Things happen in institutions.

I was in the ward because my husband and I had the opportunity to go to London for a weekend. We were young, broke; he was trying to make it as a stand-up comic. He had been hired by the BBC to appear on a late-night comedy show. I was six months pregnant. The day after we arrived, I went into preterm labor, and though we had packed for two nights, it would be six months before we would return to the United States with our son, Jack.

So, it was a difficult time. I would go into more detail here but it's a long story—almost three hundred pages long, as a matter of fact. I wrote about it in my memoir, *An Innocent, a Broad* (available wherever fine, middling-seller books are sold).

I was admitted to University College Hospital in London. We learned later that we were quite lucky that Jack was born in this particular National Health Service Hospital as it has one of the best neonatal units in the world. But at the time, I was too busy crying and fretting and torturing myself for choosing to accompany Denis on the trip. I was told I must remain on bed rest, there at that hospital, until the baby was born. They would try to prevent the onset of labor for as long as possible.

It was 1990. We didn't have cell phones. We didn't have laptops. There were no TVs in the maternity ward; it would have been annoying if there had been, given that there were eight of us in one room. But my point is, there was nothing to distract me from my obsessive rumination, the persistent why, why, why?

Why me? Why us? Why did I get on the plane? Why did I carry my suitcase?

I tried to read but couldn't focus on more than one word at a time. I flipped through magazines, stared at pictures. Why? Why?

Why? Also, I couldn't stop crying, which was annoying to the other patients and medical staff.

Finally, one of the nurses, a very pretty, soft-spoken Irish girl named Claire, informed me that I needed something to keep me busy. She thought knitting might relax me. She would teach me how. The next night, she brought me knitting needles and yarn, and in between chart notations and blood-pressure readings, she sat beside my bed and showed me how to knit.

"First, you tie a knot, just like this," she said, and she fastened a little knot on one of the long plastic knitting needles. "Then you have to cast on the first row." She held her thumb and index finger up and showed me how to take the needle and push it up with the thumb, over the tip of the needle, and then down to rest along the index finger.

"Oh, wouldn't it be lovely to have a jumper that you knit yourself for your little one?" she asked, repeating the loop-finger-thumb procedure. She crisscrossed the little tips of the needles, back and forth, back and forth, until she had a row of tidy loops lined up on one of the needles.

"I'll be right back, now, you hold this," she said, scurrying off to attend to a patient, and I sat with the needles in my hands, blinking at the tiny row of loops. When she returned, I carefully handed the needles and yarn back to her and she began, effortlessly, to knit.

Since that time, I've indulged in many things that are considered therapeutic. I've cuddled babies, watched the birth of a foal. I've meditated, bathed in spas, had "healing" massages, but nothing has ever soothed me quite the way that watching Nurse

Claire knitting soothed me that night in that strange, lonely ward. She spoke as she knit, describing her home in Belfast and her flat in Maida Vale. The language she spoke was English, but the way she pronounced the words was Irish—they were pretty words, spoken quietly, with a sweet breathiness that accompanied the consonants. The way she pronounced the word "knitting," not "nidding" as we Americans say, but "knitting." With that sweet breathiness. Her fingers were so delicate.

The gentle stabbing of the needles, the clear clacking sound as they met, and the graceful arching patterns performed by Claire's hands lulled me into a sort of trance. She knit a few rows and talked about her mother, who had taught her to knit as a little girl; her roommate, who was French; her dislike of all fish except for salmon; the weather; the royals. I wasn't crying anymore. I was melting into the music created by her voice and the tapping of the needles.

"There," she said, after knitting a few rows, "now you have a go."

"Please," I begged, "don't stop. I need to watch you knit a little more, then I'll get the hang of it."

She clickety-clacked away, describing her flatmates and a party they had thrown the night before for a friend who was moving back to Ireland. I looked around me. Though I had been in the ward for days, I was suddenly seeing it for the first time. Visiting hours were over; the boyfriends and husbands had all gone home. We were all women now. In the bed next to me, a nurse was strapping a fetal heart monitor around a pregnant belly, and then the room was filled with the swoosh, swoosh, swoosh of a baby's heart beating, many fathoms deep. I touched my belly and my own small baby rolled leisurely against my hand.

"Your turn," Claire said, trying once again to hand the knitting off to me.

"Just let me watch a little more. I think I'm starting to understand it. I just need to watch." I whispered. "Just a little more."

And she began a new row. Tap, tap, tap. Clickety, clickety, clickety, click.

"It's only tricky at the start," she said. "Soon you'll be knitting away without so much as a glance at what you're doing."

As she came to the end of each row, I feared she would try to hand the whole thing back to me. I didn't want her to stop, so I asked her about her brothers and sisters. I asked about her boyfriends. My eyes never left her hands, which began moving faster, her little fingertips tamping the yarn, the needles sliding up, down, up, down. It wasn't that I forgot where I was. I didn't forget my predicament—that would have been impossible. Instead, I found myself in a place I had not fully understood until that moment. I felt I belonged there in that room, there with the soft conversations of women all around me, there, next to the gentle swoosh, swoosh swoosh of an unborn heart. There, watching sweet Claire, knitting something warm.

PLANET MOM

If you're a young parent and want your children to know nothing about your childhood, you should talk about it all the time—that's what my father did, and I never had any questions about him or his family. When I ask my mother about her youth, which I've done all my life, she insists that she remembers almost nothing about it. The earliest photos of her that I saw when I was a child were taken when she was a young bride and then a young mother. She seemed to have alighted on this earth a fully formed adult—apparently from Planet Mom.

I'm nosy, so as a kid, I often pressed Mom for something—anything—about her formative years, and she'd offer one of a handful of anecdotes, always told in the exact same way. They were like the origin stories the KGB created for Cold War spies who needed to pass as American citizens. Mom's childhood stories were, and still are, few and vague, but they contain just enough detail to convince me that she probably was a child, once.

I have an older brother and a younger sister, and after almost half a century of interrogations (mainly conducted by me), the Judy file is still quite thin.

Here's everything I knew about my mother's "childhood" when I was growing up:

Judy (hereafter referred to as "Mom") was born in Chicago in 1939 to Mary and Eugene Sullivan. She had a brother who was much older than she. Her brother was named Eugene after their father, but everybody called him Buzzy. Her parents, Eugene and Mary, divorced when Mom was around two, and at some point, Buzzy was killed in a car accident, so Mom was raised as an only child.

Mom lived with her mother in an old farmhouse in a rural corner of northeastern Pennsylvania. Mom didn't feel that she fit in among the Future Farmers of America set during her school years there. Fortunately, she spent her summers, many weekends, and every school holiday visiting her father, Eugene, and her stepmother, Marie, at their home in New York City. These visits were magical for Judy because, as she told me many times, "Daddy and I were always so close." "Daddy" took Judy to Manhattan art museums and dinners at the 21 Club. He loved taking her out and showing her off.

"But what about your mother?" I used to ask.

We knew our mother's father and his second wife, Marie. We visited them once a year at their home in Staten Island, and they visited us in the Midwest. They seemed grouchy and a little frightening to me, so I wasn't that curious about them. I wanted to know about my grandmother, whom I barely remembered, though she lived until I had children of my own.

Mom and her mother simply didn't like one another, she explains to this day, without the slightest hint of sadness or anger. When I ask her to elaborate, she says that she avoided her mother as much as possible when she was a child. Mom used to climb up onto a special boulder in the woods next to their house where she loved to sit and read for hours. Oh, and at one point, she and her mother lived with a relative in Scranton, where Mom enjoyed roller-skating to the library.

Those stories are the chicken scratch my mother tossed me, her nosiest child, every time I interrogated her. The boulder, the lonely farmhouse, the razzle-dazzle nights with Daddy in the Big Apple. Oh, and roller-skating in Scranton.

When I ask Mom why she didn't like her mother, her answer is that her mother was awful—so awful she refused to attend my mother's wedding to my father. Yeah, that's awful is what I've always thought. When I used to ask about Buzzy, her brother, Mom had even less to offer. She didn't know very much about him because of the vast age difference and his early death. I had the impression he was a teenager when she was a baby or toddler.

I must be careful here, because even though I was under that impression, I can't say that my mother ever told me how old she was when he died. I was often trying to fill in the blanks regarding Mom, because she'd shrouded her childhood in such secrecy. So I might have connected the wrong dots. She said that he died when she was young, but youth is relative. I knew he was an older teen or young adult when he died, because he was driving the car that killed him in the crash. Mom said that she never grieved her brother's loss, because Buzzy, like my grandmother, was never very nice to her. My mother's heart belonged to "Daddy." Everything happy about her childhood came from him. Everything bad was caused by her mother—my grandmother Mary.

Still, when I was a child, even though I only met my grandmother a few times, I felt a strong affinity toward her. I thought the part of Pennsylvania where my grandmother lived was magical. Children aren't great real-estate appraisers; I didn't notice the area had seen better days. I saw horses and cows in some of the weedy fields near her ramshackle farmhouse and I was obsessed with horses. There were farms and woods and streams nearby. It felt like something out of a storybook; it was so green and hilly, the air so fresh, the sky so blue. For perspective, we lived in a charmless, treeless subdivision in Midland, Michigan, under what seemed like a constant acid rain–filled cloud produced by the chemical company, where pretty much everybody in the town—including my father—worked. When we were at my grandmother's, I fantasized about being one of my favorite literary characters—Heidi. My quiet, frowning grandmother didn't live in the Swiss Alps, but I was sure that if I were allowed to live with her in this fresh-aired, pony-permitting paradise, I'd be able to jolly her out of her darkness and show her what love was all about.

During those visits, I gleaned that my grandmother was self-conscious, shy, and nervous—rather like me—but also outdoorsy, a little messy, and seemingly more comfortable around animals than people—just like me! Also, we almost shared a birthday. My grandmother was born on August 15. I was born on August 14, and my mother used to joke about pushing me out on that day so I wouldn't have to share the same birthday as her mother, who, again, she loathed. I think Mom's loathing also contributed to the imagined kinship I felt toward my grandmother (Granny? Grandma? I don't recall). My mother hated her mother. And, while I knew that my mother loved me in some ways, I also sensed that she hated me in others. Of course, I hated her right back—and loved her intensely. I know now that this love/hate dynamic isn't unusual between mothers and daughters. In her popular book *My Mother, My Self,* Nancy Friday wrote: "When I stopped seeing my mother with the eyes of a child, I saw the woman who helped me give birth to myself." My mother was self-taught when it came to parenting—her mom had been raised by nuns in an orphanage and wasn't much of a role model. Somehow my mother taught herself how to be quite an amazing mother.

When I was about eight, Mom flew from our home in Michigan to Pennsylvania to be with her mother, who had just been hospitalized for reasons unknown to us kids. Within a day or two, Mom flew back home, reporting that her mother had been so awful to her that she was never going to speak to her again.

And she didn't. My grandmother lived for decades after this incident, but my brother, sister, and I never saw her or spoke to her again. The idea that my mother could so coolly sever ties with her own mother because of "awful" behavior was frightening to me, to put it mildly, because my mother often described my behavior as awful. Every time she stormed out of a room or slammed a door between us, part of me thought I'd never see her again. Of course, I did. She was our mother, and though I tested her with plenty of "awful" behavior, she stuck around. There were times, many times, when I wished she would vanish from my life in the same way that she had vanished from her mother's, and then I would be consumed with fear that something terrible would happen to her. Our relationship was always so fraught. I felt that there was a key to understanding her and was sure it had to do with her childhood.

Happy Days was a popular TV show when I was young. It was about a group of fun-loving, attractive high school kids in the 1950s, which was when my mother was in high school. I used to ask Mom if she, like the teens on the show, wore poodle skirts and saddle shoes, if she went to sock hops or knew any cool "greasers" who drove hot rods and started rumbles. She responded with vague affirmatives. "Yes, we all did things like that." Then, if pressed, she described the boulder in the woods where she read her books. Roller-skating in Scranton. She said it was sometimes lonely in the country, but she's never dwelled on that because she spent all her free time tripping the light fantastic in New York with Daddy.

Years later, during a trip I took with my mother to look at colleges, I learned that Mom's brother, Buzzy, hadn't died when my mother was little. The strained relationship between my mother and me resolved itself when I became old enough to drink with her. Not old enough to legally drink—the drinking age was eighteen. But my mother and I became drinking buddies when I was around sixteen, and she was newly divorced. My mother wouldn't go to the popular restaurants or bars in our small town by herself.

Only alcoholics drink alone, Mom taught me. They drink alone, at home.

I learned, while drinking with my mother, that her own mother was a real alcoholic—she drank alone at home and in bars. My grandmother would go weeks or even months without touching alcohol, but then she'd go on a "toot" and be drunk for days. Mom had been afraid to invite friends to her home after school because her mother might be passed out on the floor. Her mother had a reputation. She wasn't just a divorcée in a small town during a time when divorces were still scandalous. She was a drunk. When my mother was very little, a girl who lived across the street told her that she was forbidden to play with my mother because my grandmother was "bad." At that time, my grandfather was serving in WWII, my grandmother was working most days, and the whole neighborhood could see the groceries that were left on her porch on delivery day. Apparently, Granny ordered a lot of beer for a young mother whose husband was away.

Unlike my grandmother, Mom never has a drink before five o'clock, unless it's a lunch where everybody is having a drink, or she's on vacation. She would never enter a bar or restaurant alone and order a drink. That's what keeps her in the "social drinking" category. When I was a teenager in the late 1970s, my newly single and very pretty mother would go out with her many fun friends or, as a last resort—me. That's when Mom and I bonded. Some people get meaner when they drink. My mother gets nicer. The more she drinks, the softer and kinder she becomes. The polite but sometimes brittle guardedness that is her baseline sober state seems to dissipate with each cocktail, and I was always happy to lap up all the love and vodka tonics on our nights out together.

One night, when my mother and I were in upstate New York looking at colleges, we had a few drinks in a restaurant, and I learned that my uncle Buzzy didn't die when Mom was a little girl. He died when she was twenty—just two months before her wedding. He was only four years older than my mother. She'd grown up with a living sibling. Years later, thanks to the internet and digital newspaper archives, I learned more. Uncle Buzzy had violent, criminal tendencies from the time he was a small child; my mother was terrified in her own house because of him. When Buzzy died in a drunk-driving wreck, at twenty-four, he'd packed a lot into his short life. He'd lied about his age and enlisted in the army when he was fifteen. He had spent some of his high school years in boot camp, then in Germany before being discharged for reasons unknown. He got his GED and attended college for a year. He married twice and had a child with each young woman. At age twenty-one, he embezzled a large sum of money from a hardware store where he worked.

When his thievery was discovered, he came home drunk and went down to their cellar for his guns, threatened his young wife with a pistol, then left town in an attempt to evade police.

The newspaper headline for his arrest in Pennsylvania later that night read: PISTOL PACKING FUGITIVE TAKEN BY CITY POLICE. He'd staggered into a bar in Sunbury, Pennsylvania, with his hand inside his raincoat. A suspicious patron knocked his arm and a pistol fell onto the floor. There was a scuffle, and when the police arrived, they found his car was filled with handguns and rifles, some registered, some not. He served time in Terre Haute penitentiary and was released at least a year before he died.

This was my mother's brother. I'd never seen his picture, but I found photos of him online along with the news items about his crimes and his death. Mom says she never knew about Buzzy's marriages or children, but she's been more willing to talk about him in recent years. She wrote to him while he was in prison, she told me, when I asked her about his arrests. I once asked her if Buzzy had shown antisocial traits as a child. What I meant was, did she think he was born a sociopath. She thought I was asking if he was shy. She said that no, he was very outgoing. Even though he liked to bully her, he always knew how to charm other people. As he got older, he was especially charming to women. So, yes, it seems Uncle Buzzy had some sociopathic traits. Poor Mom.

If you meet my mother, never pity her. She'll laugh at such absurdity and explain that she's very, very happy, she always has been. She doesn't like to think about the past all the time; she's not obsessed with herself or relatives she's never met, like *some people*. She lives in the present.

A few years ago, I learned more about the trip Mom took to visit her mother in the hospital when I was a child—the visit that culminated in my mother permanently severing ties with her own mother. My grandmother was in the hospital because she'd attempted suicide. My grandmother was not just an alcoholic; she had what was then called manic depression but is now known as bipolar disorder. She had tried to kill herself several times. My grandmother's life had been filled with trauma. She'd been raised by nuns in an orphanage; she was abandoned by her husband with two small children and no money. She had no idea what normal mothers and families were like. It seems that she tried her best, but she filled her own children's lives with chaos and trauma. Ultimately, my mother cut the twisted cord that connected us, the children she was doing her best to raise like "normal" children, from my grandmother, who wasn't "normal."

Still, in the years after sharing all this, Mom maintains that the only times she thinks about her mother or brother are when I'm pestering her; otherwise, she has few thoughts or memories of her childhood. There was the boulder, the roller-skating, the wonderful trips to the city—oh—here's another. My grandmother and her second husband, Charlie, kept hunting dogs—I believe they were beagles. My mother once told me that when she was young, she was given some chicks for Easter one year. The chicks liked to flock around one of the beagles and nestle up against her for warmth. The dog, a female, who'd born litters, was stirred by their helplessness and she began to treat them as if they were her own puppies, herding them about with her nose and even lifting them delicately in her soft mouth. Then, in some kind of haywire hormone surge, the dog produced milk for the baby birds. Apparently, everybody was amazed at this biological wonder, but when I asked for more details—what happened to the milk? Did the chicks try to nurse? Mom shrugged and said, "Who knows. They were just animals. I doubt they gave it much thought."

I know she's right, but the story always saddened me. Something about all the misguided love. The poor dog, her nipples painfully engorged and leaking, trying to pull the chicks close with her soft muzzle, and the confused chicks with nothing but the fuzzy recollection of a lost mother's downy breast, huddled against the only warm thing they can find.

BATMAN

I was watching one of the morning "news" shows recently, and as they cut away to a commercial, the female anchor said, "Coming up, the words no mother wants to hear from her child." This interested me because I had already heard the words no mother wants to hear from her child. These words are: "Mom, there's a bat on your pajamas."

It was early morning when I heard the words; this was years ago, when our kids were young and we lived in Connecticut, but I remember it like it was yesterday. I was sitting at our dining room table in my pajamas, talking on the phone and writing something down. Our nine-year-old daughter, Devin, came downstairs. I stood up for some reason, still nattering away, and she said, "Mom! Mom! Mom! Mom!"

I snapped my fingers and frowned—the universal mother's sign language for "Shut your damn trap, I'm on the phone."

"MOM," Devin said again, her voice rising now. I looked at her, and that's when she said, staring down at my thigh and backing up, "Mom, there's a . . . bat on . . . your . . . pajamas!"

Time stood still then. I was staring at Devin, heart racing, the phone held to my ear. Later, we would puzzle over my eventual response, which was, "Is it real?"

For some reason, I was whispering and looking intensely into Devin's eyes when I said this. I couldn't bring myself to look down at my pajamas.

"YES!" Devin screamed. I had to look down, and there it was—clinging to my threadbare, paper-thin pajama bottoms—a furry, hideously ugly, maniacally grinning brown bat. He gripped my pajamas with claws that came out of—was it possible? Yes, the claws were attached to his disgusting wings. He was leering up at me with his half-human/half-pig face, and the next thing I knew I was standing at the opposite end of our house screaming and clinging to Devin, who was also screaming. In our flight through the house, I had somehow managed to brush my demonically cheerful, pug-nosed passenger from my pajamas (and drop the phone), and Devin and I just stood there, clinging to each other, alternately shrieking, laughing, and crying.

When we'd bought that little Connecticut farm, we'd been aware of the area's bat population and were pleased that our property was inhabited by so many of these useful creatures. According to an article in the local paper, a single brown bat can devour between three thousand and seven thousand mosquitoes in one night. At dusk, Denis and I used to watch them fly out from under the eaves of our old barn and dart about the sky, and we would gaze up at our little mosquito-assassins and smile. In our minds, there was a beautiful symbiosis between the bats and the Learys. We owned the property but were willing to allow the bats to live on it. In return, they would kill all the mosquitoes so that we could sometimes eat our supper outside. We lived under the misconception that there was a mutually understood, unwritten treaty clearly defining the boundaries of our territories. The bats got the whole outside. The only place off-limits to them was the inside of our house. We knew that bats sometimes carry rabies, but what we didn't know was that up close, a bat's creepiness quotient is off the charts, and, like a terrorist, it doesn't set much store by boundaries. It rules through fear and intimidation and travels about with the smug knowledge that it can go anywhere it damn well pleases. And it does.

I'm a little embarrassed that we had so many bat invasions. We went through a long period when we kept forgetting to close the chimney flue. If you're new to country living, please take my advice and never leave the chimney flue open in the summertime. The first time we did this, we were in a rented house. It was before we moved up to the country full-time and were not so wise about the wild things that fly and crawl and slither into country houses at all hours. Our children were very young—maybe three and five years old, and our friends Ted and Amanda were visiting for the weekend. Long story short—I left the flue open and after dinner we saw something fluttering around the living room.

"I wonder what that is," Denis mused. Then the thing came fluttering into the dining room, aiming straight for Denis's head, and all hell broke loose. The rapid-fire tragic-comic stunt sequence that followed included (but was not limited to) Denis trampling our children; Denis using the most foul language imaginable in front of our children; and Denis nearly knocking the very pregnant Amanda down a flight of stairs.

It occurred to me during those frantic moments that until that night, I had never seen Denis genuinely afraid. During our years in the city, his courage had certainly been put to the test. There was the night, for example, when I woke up with the spine-chilling suspicion that there was another person in the apartment. I poked Denis awake and he grabbed a baseball bat and searched each room, tapping the thick of it against his palm. Another time an agitated homeless crack-addict guy approached with violent taunts on the street and Denis assuaged him with a cigarette. His bravery was most admirably on display when our building became infested with mice and he would walk ahead of me into the kitchen, while I clung to him, my face buried in his back, whining, "Do you see any? Do you see any?" I had watched Denis stand up to Harvey Weinstein, out-curse a frenzied cabby, and once, when a snarling pit bull came barreling toward us in the park, Denis, who loves dogs, began slapping his thigh, and before I knew it, he and the dog were playfully rolling around on the ground together. What I didn't know then was that every man has something that makes his blood run cold. For Humphrey Bogart in *The African Queen*, it was leeches. For Denis, it's bats.

Another memorable home invasion occurred when Denis was fortunately (for him) out of town. My kids were around middle school age then, and one evening, we were watching TV when I thought I saw something whiz above my head. Sure enough, it was another bat. Devin, Jack, and I leapt from the couch screaming, and it soared—well, they don't really soar, they do fighter-jet maneuvers, twisting, diving, spiraling, but it did perform a horrifying airshow above us. It swooped in Devin's direction at one point, and she did what anybody would do in her position—she literally pulled the rug from under our feet, placed it on her head, then screamed and ran in circles. My son, being over six feet tall in ninth grade, felt like an easy target, so he assumed a squatting position and sped across the living room in a sort of crab-walk, bellowing about rabies. I chose to cling to my son, who, even squatting, is taller than me, so I felt that he was a human shield. I have strong maternal instincts, but in times like this, it really is every man for himself.

Finally, we decided to flee the house and we sat in my car, huddled together like three terrified, twitching rabbits. We left the door to the house open, hoping the bat would leave rather than send a sonar invite to his friends flying outside, and from the car we watched the bat put on a show that was clearly meant to shock and awe. First it swooped back and forth through our living room, our dogs chasing it and leaping at it. Then it landed on the floor and staggered around, dragging its disgusting form across our rug with its clawed wings. When it did this the dogs stopped chasing it and began looking for us, proving that even dogs are horrified by bats when they get a close-enough look. Finally, the bat found its way out the door.

Within days, we had a metal "cap" placed over the chimney. It let smoke out but didn't allow bats in. We knew where the bats lived—they were in a tiny crawl space above our attic ceiling. We saw dozens of them fly out of their little air vent each night. We saw the stain of their droppings on the white clapboards up there, which was kind of gross, but this setup was fine, we never used the crawl space.

A few years later, we decided to have our bathroom redone.

First, the shower needed to be fixed, and then we determined that the shower needed to be replaced, and before long we had a contractor in who suggested we have the entire bathroom gutted and rebuilt. The contractor wanted to expose beams and make a vaulted ceiling. As he pointed to the area of the ceiling that he would be destroying, I realized that the area above it contained our chamber of bat horrors.

"I don't like the idea of opening that up," I said. "We've had issues with bats."

"No problem," said Joseph, the contractor. "It just opens up to the crawl space, not the outdoors."

"I know, but we have bats in the crawl space."

I was then treated to a lecture on how bats, even in an enclosed crawl space, can kill your family and topple your house. They carry disease, said Joseph, they have some kind of spore in their "guana." (Suddenly Joseph was a zoologist and couldn't say "bat shit" like everybody else.)

It was determined that the whole project would be put off until we had the bats removed. I asked around and got the name of the best wildlife-removal professional in our area. Denis and I could never remember his name, so we referred to him as Batman.

It was early spring when we called Batman. He came out and informed us that in addition to the attic crawl space, we had bats under all our eaves and behind many loose shingles. He wanted to get rid of the bats immediately by placing a loose net over our entire house. This way, the bats could fly out but not back in. But it had to be done right away; the bats would be having babies in a few weeks. If Batman sealed them from the house after the babies were born, the mothers wouldn't be able to return to them and the babies would die. He started to explain what a stinky situation that would be, but he had already lost me with the words "mothers" and "dead babies."

"Are the mothers pregnant now?" I asked Batman.

"Yes," he said. "So you really need to get them out before they have the babies."

"But where will they go? What if they can't find another unoccupied attic in time?" I said, because even pig-faced, flying rodents become precious to me when I'm forced to consider their babies. My attic was, in fact, a bat nursery, and I had to think of the mothers, all plump and expectant, all warm and safe, hanging by their toes from the ceiling. No, I decided, the bats must be allowed to remain in the attic until after the babies were born and able to fly. Then Batman could put his net over the house.

Well, spring came and went, and Batman became very busy, but we decided there was no rush. The bathroom was going to cost a small fortune. The shower wasn't so bad. We'd wait until the fall, when the bats flew south for the winter. Life would be saner then. Jack would be heading off to college, and I'd have more time to focus on it all. We passed the summer watching the bats soaring and dipping over the fields each evening, and I must admit that I began to feel a sense of proud ownership toward them. These bats had all been born and bred in my own house and they were a fine-looking bunch. *These Leary bats are special*, I told myself, then I screamed and shuddered and ran into the barn when one swooped a little too close to my head.

Toward the end of the summer, we got another call from Batman. If we wanted the bats out by winter, now was the time. They would be hibernating soon. I had thought bats were migratory, for some reason, and when I heard that they hibernate, visions of sleeping bear cubs came to my mind—visions of warm, cuddly, sleeping mammals.

"Where will they go?"

"Someplace else!" Batman cried.

The man's job is to get rid of bats, and he was losing his patience with me. I was having a hard time letting go. They weren't just any bats now; they were our bats. I imagined our bat families returning from an evening of mosquito bingeing, only to find their beloved home impenetrable. I imagined them flying from house to house, knocking on eaves and loose clapboards, only to be driven off by the territorial winged residents already there (and bats hate those bat houses—we had them all over our property—it's the one place where bats won't roost). I imagined them huddled in a tree, the mother's frozen wing wrapped around her young, the father wringing his ghastly claws in despair, and the little ones squeaking, "Why can't we go back in the warm house?"

"Because the selfish witch lady wants the whole place to herself, dear one."

"We'll wait until next spring," I told Batman. "Let's wait until the early spring, before they have their babies."

We decided the bathroom was fine the way it was. The bats' free lease of our crawl space was extended for the time being. We put off some other home repairs, either because of the expense, the wildlife, or the chaos that the remodeling stage would create in our lives. "We'll wait until Jack's gone off to school," we said about a section of our roof that needed new shingles. "The roof problem is above his room—what if the repairs cause a leak?" As Jack prepared to leave the nest, we sighed and said, "Let's wait until Devin goes to college, that's only two more years."

Jack left for college, and during Devin's last two years of high school, Denis was often working and staying in the city during the week. When it was just Devin and me at home, most of the household rules fell by the wayside. Family dinners had always been an important time, but Devin usually had plans after school, so we ate whenever we could—often not together.

Denis and I have a king-sized bed, and the kids and I always loved watching movies and favorite shows from that bed, surrounded by our dogs and snacks and drinks. During those last couple of years, Devin would bring in her books and homework and we'd work side by side. Often, if we didn't have too much work, we'd watch movies late into the night.

One night, I decided it was time for Devin to watch a movie that I treasure above almost any other—*Grey Gardens*. I'm talking about the classic—the original documentary by the Maysles brothers. It's about an elderly mother and her middle-aged daughter ("Big Edie" and "Little Edie" Beale), who were closely related to Jackie Onassis. They had once been beautiful and very wealthy. Now this wildly eccentric pair lived in their falling-down mansion—Grey Gardens—in the most exclusive estate area of the Hamptons, surrounded by squalor, their fortune gone, the decrepit house overrun with cats, raccoons, and fleas. I've seen it dozens of times. I've always been madly in love with the Edies, and since they were mother and daughter, I thought it would be a great bonding experience to share the film with my own daughter.

Devin and I arranged ourselves in the bed as usual and started watching. As I had hoped, she loved it as much as I did. We rewound and played, again and again, the moments when the filmmakers showed the younger, more beautiful versions of the women. They were so fascinating, so wonderfully eccentric, such delightful messes, these Beales. *Oh my God*, we cried, when Big Edie offered corn on the cob to the film crew from her filthy bed.

I asked Devin to pass me the chicken—we sometimes had dinner in bed that winter. When she reached for it, she found that our dog Daphne was trying to devour it.

"Well, is anything left?" I asked. I was starving.

Daphne had gotten a thigh, but not the drumstick, and after Dev wrestled it from the dog's jaws, I brushed it off and ate it. Devin discovered the bag of chips we'd opened the night before, behind one of the pillows, and we ate those too, smiling indulgently at the antics of the wonderful, eccentric Beales.

"EEEEEDIIIIIE!" Big Edie shrieked, whenever little Edie left her room. "EEEEEEDIE!"

"That's what you sound like when you call me," Devin chortled.

"What?" I laughed. "I don't!"

We were thirsty, so I paused the movie while Devin went downstairs to get us some drinks. I wanted dessert.

"DEVIN," I called. No answer.

"DEEEEEEEEVIIIIIIIIIN!" I called again.

She brought up the drinks and a big carton of ice cream, and we dug in and restarted the movie. She didn't mention that I had just done the very thing I said I never did. I'd Big Edie'd her. She knew that I wasn't trying to be funny. That I'd only realized I was doing it when I did it, and that it was a little embarrassing for me. We continued watching until Big Edie offered the film crew a taste of her liquefied ice cream. Devin's dripping spoon paused midair; the ice cream carton nestled between us. She looked at me. She looked around the room.

"I have to finish writing a paper," she said, grabbing the paper plates and ice cream carton and leaping from the bed.

"No, stay," I said. "DEVIIIIN! Write it in here!"

"It's due tomorrow," she called, without looking back.

I paused the movie. Fine, we'd finish watching it another night.

It was disappointing, though. I'd wanted to hear Devin's take on the Beales: How had they ended up the way they did? I mean, what exactly was wrong with them? Little Edie appeared to have some kind of mood disorder, but maybe she'd just been driven to the brink of madness by her wildly narcissistic mother. Why didn't she leave already; go make a life for herself? Why did she and her mother, who'd once been so glamorous, choose to live like hermits in that falling-down pile of a house? They'd always had strong opinions about society and men—had they let themselves and their house go out of anger toward Mr. Beale, or out of spite toward the snobby town? Did the raccoons and cats drive him away?

I heard a scratching noise above me. The bats . . .

Why were the bats still here?

I jumped up, shooed the dogs from the bed, and began to straighten the covers. Would I start feeding those disgusting bats, the way the Beales fed the raccoons that'd taken over their attic? Why had they let raccoons take over the attic?

It was then that I saw how a gradual decline could have happened to the Edies without them even being aware of it. They'd fix things later, they kept promising, only later never arrived. The house became embarrassing, but they kept putting things off, just as we'd been doing, waiting until this happened or that happened. Meanwhile, they adapted themselves to each level of Grey Gardens' decline: their world grew smaller, they saw people less and less . . . and animals become their closest friends and neighbors. Finally, the house was condemned and, in a sense, so were they.

I called Batman the next day.

Devin and I did watch the rest of *Grey Gardens* eventually, and we've since watched it many times. But not until after Batman, the roofer, and Contractor Joseph came back and helped restore us, and our home, to something resembling sanity.

THE DEEP, DARK ME

This morning, I helped a friend wage war against a major insurance company that was trying to deny coverage of her husband's heart surgery. I also signed a petition supporting a political candidate and pledged a small donation to that candidate's campaign. After lunch, I visited the Pennsylvania State Archives to research historical information for a book talk I'm giving. I shopped for paper towels, dog food, and other household supplies, paid a few bills, and checked in with a group of friends that I chat with daily. Then I worked on a social media marketing strategy with my publisher.

It's three o'clock. I've already "engaged" with 16,325 people, and the day is still young. I've done all of this "engagement" in my bed, on my computer. I've actually not spoken a word to anybody but my dogs in several days. My sink is filled with dirty dishes. I need a shower. The thousands of people I "engaged" with, according to my Facebook stats, are those who visited my author page. There they saw my smiling, professionally enhanced author photo. They saw my photoshopped, near perfect hair. They read the short "status update" that I edited twice after I posted it this morning.

On the internet, I'm friendly, thoughtful, and altruistic. I'm a doer, a go-getter, a fun-loving "people person" whose looks have held up relatively well for my age. In real life, I'm a borderline hermit who is slovenly, pessimistic, and wrinkled. If you look at me in the daylight, you'll see that I have peach fuzz dusting my chin. I need to go to the post office, but I've been putting it off all day. I've become increasingly uncomfortable seeing people out and about. I prefer my internet persona to the real-life me, and who wouldn't? She's better.

My internet self, the "virtual" me, probably began to eclipse the flesh-and-blood version long before Covid, though it's my habit to blame everything on Covid now. It likely began soon after my publisher suggested I join Facebook sometime in 2008 to help publicize a forthcoming novel. Later, I joined Twitter, Instagram, Pinterest, and Reddit. I've made many friends on social media. Some are also friends in real life, but others remain virtual friends. I have some virtual friends who know more about me than people I've known all my life.

For example, the group I mentioned that I chat with online? There are five of us who are regulars, though others check in occasionally. We text each other almost daily on Facebook Messenger. We all live in the greater New York area, but I only knew one member of the group in real life when we all started hanging out online. We came together because we shared a mutual fascination with an internet fraud. Not a garden-variety fake like the rest of us.

She doesn't just post photoshopped selfies. She doesn't just remove embarrassing photos that relatives have posted on her Facebook page. This woman (let's call her Jane) is the real deal.

Let me stop here and say that when I first became fascinated with Jane, I had an excuse. It was research. I'd spent the past two years writing a novel about a young woman who is famous on the internet. On her popular mommy blog, she's snarky, busy, hilarious, and totally relatable to her millions of followers. In real life, she's a shy recluse with no children. She lives alone with her mother. So, I'm interested in online frauds. I'm terrified of Jane, so I won't go into too much detail here. I suspect many people will think they know who I'm writing about, but I think our Jane is probably better.

Our Jane has connections to the CIA. Yes, so do many pathological liars. But our Jane also has close ties to NASA, the Democratic National Committee, and Comedy Central. She's a beautiful Manhattan socialite who does relief work with refugees. I no longer follow Jane, but when I did, she had almost one hundred thousand Twitter followers. She updated her Facebook status many times a day. If a few hours went by and she hadn't posted something, it was because she'd been at the UN addressing a panel of world leaders or in the hospital on life support. She struggled with several life-threatening diseases, but she was a trooper. She had money issues, due to her illnesses and her abusive former husband. She posted links to her "Wish List" on Amazon, in case anybody was interested. During Fashion Week, she flitted from one show to another with her celebrity friends. She schooled us on how to behave on a red carpet. She needed to get rid of some clutter and wondered what to do with an old Chanel bag. She was strapped for cash—the bag was a gift from a boyfriend. Maybe she'd sell it to one of her Facebook "friends." It would sure help with her medical and legal bills.

How much? her Facebook friends wrote in the comments.

SELL IT TO ME! they'd post.

We love you, Jane!

A friend who shared my fascination with Jane introduced me to a group that had begun to discuss her on Facebook Messenger. In the beginning we just texted every now and then, usually after a particularly preposterous claim or another post grifting for money or gifts. Jane sometimes launched brutal cyberattacks on the few people who dared question the veracity of her posts. We were amazed at how many people seemed to believe her. We all had online connections with Jane—she and I shared over one hundred mutual friends on Facebook, though nobody I knew had ever met her. Some of the people who "liked" and commented on her status updates were well-known journalists, doctors, and lawyers.

Jane unwittingly gave clues daily that she didn't live in or even near New York City. She was lazy with her lying. She'd post that she was getting red-carpet ready for a gala and then, two hours later, post a tipsy update revealing that she was watching *Sex and the City* reruns at home alone. How had the others not seen through her lies? More important, why did we care?

The point of my story isn't really Jane—it's the group of us who were so fascinated with her. Each of us are moderately intelligent. We all went to college. We all have families and jobs. Yet we devoted hours of our time to watching and discussing this stranger we were all "friends" with on social media. Jane did help me flesh out the character in my novel, especially when our suspicions were confirmed and we learned that she's actually an unemployed single mother who lives in the Midwest and may or may not be, as we had long suspected, engaged in illegal activity.

But eventually, we weren't really talking about Jane anymore; we had just gotten into the habit of connecting with each other every day. I shared things with this group that my closest friends don't know about me. Jane reminded some of us of our mothers or stepmothers. She reminded us of childhood mean girls. She found her way into our dreams and our work. We discussed all of this via text messages. We had running jokes. We greeted each other with Bitmojis and other silliness.

But here's the strange thing—when we did finally meet in real life, we five who had become so intimate with each other online, it was a little uncomfortable. We had texted daily for months. But now, seated together at a table in a Manhattan restaurant, we realized that we sat among strangers. We struggled with small talk. We caught each other up on our work and our families. We joked about politics. But the conversation felt somewhat forced. There were little awkward silences. I remember worrying that the peach fuzz on my chin was visible. I covered my chin with my hand.

Eventually, one of us glanced at their phone and announced that Jane had just posted something new. We whipped out our phones. We all started typing at once. Now she was starting her own fashion line! We posted funny GIFs to each other about the waitress who was ignoring us. We told the one man in the group that he needed a better Bitmoji, and we all sent him our ideas. When our food arrived, we dined happily, a group of dear friends, reunited at last. We passed around our phones, sharing photos of our children and pets. We ignored the strangers sitting next to us and embraced the people we had grown to love—there, in the place where we're all a little bit better, where we're all greater or lesser frauds—the internet.

THREE-DRINKS-SHORT

"May I offer you a tropical punch made with our own island rum?" asked the young hostess with the lovely West Indian accent. Then, smiling at our eleven-year-old son and nine-year-old daughter, she added, "Perhaps a fruit punch for the children?"

Denis said, "No thanks," and stepped outside for a cigarette.

I said, "Yes, the kids and I would love a fruit punch, thanks."

It had been a long trip. There was a layover in Miami, and then a slow, hot drive across another island to a boat that took us to this island, and now we had to wait for our luggage to be transported to the resort. Somehow, our bags had been sent to the wrong hotel. We had kids. We had stuff we needed. We were still dressed for the winter, but it was eighty-five degrees outside, and our room wasn't ready. Denis and I were barely speaking; the heat and exhaustion from racing through airports and tending to the children had made us revert to our favorite go-to coping device—blaming each other for everything that went wrong.

We had begun the day in Connecticut, all four of us eagerly

anticipating a relaxing week in the sun. It was late February. We had been wearing boots, coats, and mittens for months, and once I booked the flights, I had not thought much about the logistics of getting to the resort. Somehow, I'd just had a vision of my family boarding an airplane and then running and laughing, all four of us, hand in hand across a white sandy beach, and then diving into the surf where we would spend the entire week, frolicking and splashing about like a family of playful seals. I had forgotten that we had a very tight window of time between landing in Miami and boarding our flight to the island. When our flight out from JFK was delayed, we ended up missing the connecting flight and had to wait in Miami for six hours until the next one. The children were restless. Denis felt the need to repeatedly interrogate me about my mindset when I had booked the flights so close together. I silently interrogated myself about my mindset when I had decided I would marry this tyrant.

But now, finally, we were in a tropical paradise with a cheerful, accommodating receptionist. A man appeared with three drinks on a tray. Two of them were bright pink and were garnished with a pineapple wedge. The third was a paler shade of pink and it also had the pineapple garnish. The bright pink ones were handed to the kids. The third was for me. It appeared to be diluted with something. I pretended not to notice. I held my breath as I lifted the large glass to my lips so that I couldn't smell its contents. Oops. It tasted like there might be alcohol in it, but I wasn't sure, so I took another sip. Yes, it tasted like rum. I hadn't asked for the rum drink, so I took another sip to be certain. Yup, rum, all right. After all those years, I still recognized the lovely sweetness of rum and the warm way that it, like all spirits, made my heart feel as if it might overflow with goodness.

Fourteen years earlier, at the age of twenty-four, I had slunk, absolutely sodden with shame and self-loathing, into a church basement to attend a meeting for alcoholics. Yes, one of *those* meetings, stocked with men and women who gathered regularly to "share their experience, strength, and hope with each other" in order to recover from alcoholism. It's an anonymous organization that prefers that its members don't reveal their involvement in the fellowship on a public level, and most of its members call it "the Program." I had known about the Program ever since a friend's mother took me to my first meeting when I was eighteen years old. The mother was in the Program and believed, based on my drunken antics at her house, and some stories that her daughter had shared with her, that I might benefit from the Program myself. I didn't. I was too young, but I was rather fascinated to learn that a few of my friends' parents were in this depressing program where adults sat around in a circle and spoke in low tones and, at times, wept. My parents were out drinking that night, probably really tying one on, but Peggy Schumacher's mom was in the meeting drinking coffee, and so was the guy who worked in our local grocery store.

Poor Peggy Schumacher's mom, I thought. Poor guy from the market. They were alcoholics who would never be able to drink for the rest of their lives. You had to pity them.

Over the next several years, I occasionally thought about the meeting and the people there. I felt very sorry for the members of the Program, but, though part of me always knew that I drank differently than most others, I knew that I wasn't an alcoholic. I went to college, held jobs. I had lots of friends. I just needed to control my drinking. My friends all liked to drink, but somehow, on most occasions, I was the one nobody was speaking to the next day. I was a blackout drinker from the very first time I drank, in junior high school, so I often didn't have any recollection of what I had done to enrage my friends. We had all been having drinks, and I'd been feeling great, loving my friends, loving myself, repeatedly expressing my love for my fellows and myself . . . and then it was the next morning, my friends weren't speaking to me, and I hated myself again.

My friend Lauren tried to help me sort it all out one day. "The problem with you is that you just don't know when to stop. After two or three drinks, I start to get that out-of-control feeling, and I realize it's time to switch to water. I think that's what you need to do."

I remember nodding tearfully. I was reeling with shame about some incident from the night before, but in all honesty, I had no idea what she was talking about. After two or three drinks was precisely when I always started to feel *in control.* But how do you explain to a social drinker what it's like to have been born three-drinks-short of comfortable? You can't.

When I stopped drinking at age twenty-four, I went to another meeting. This time, I heard what all the other people born three-drinks-short were saying, and I realized I had found my tribe. I always loved boozers when I was drinking—I'd single them out at parties within seconds and plant myself next to them—the fun people. And now, here were the same characters, *sans* booze, but *avec* the warped perspectives, maladaptive coping skills, and hysterical stories about how they came to be in the Program. I found myself shoulder to shoulder with my brethren—all the disappointed dreamers—the type of people who imagine themselves running along beaches, holding hands with their loved ones, and then are blindsided by the logistics of getting from one place to another. I learned in the Program that I drank to cope with the disappointments of life, and that I needed meetings to help me live life on life's terms (another corny cult slogan), not based on my own childish fantasies about how life should be.

In early sobriety, there was some joy and relief each morning when I woke up and remembered having gone to bed the night before, but I missed drinking. A lot. The topography of the dry world, especially during those early months, was so strange and foreign that it was sometimes hard to find my bearings. So, like an expat who has found herself in a sometimes beautiful but often frightening new land, I liked to meet up with people from my soggy homeland and remind myself why I had left. I met writers, artists, bankers, ex-cons, current felons, grannies, junkies, and the occasional movie star at meetings of the Program that I attended. My new friends and I made fun of the corniness of the slogans and the literature, but at the same time we clung to the ridiculously simplistic tenets of the Program (*one day at a time, easy does it*), and lived by them.

"You gotta be neck-deep in this thing if you wanna get better," an aging bookie named Gino told me at one of my first meetings.

Soon I was neck-deep, and my life did get better. My relationship with Denis—at that time, my live-in boyfriend—improved. We got married, we had two great kids, Denis's career took off, and we were no longer broke. We moved to Manhattan and later to Connecticut. I had been sober about eight years (one day at a time!) when I stopped going to meetings.

There were many reasons why I stopped going. First, it was hard to find the time. When I had an hour or two away from the kids, I wanted to do other things that seemed more important. Also, I started to worry about other parents seeing me coming in and out of the church basements with the big A triangles hanging from the doors. Before I had kids, while we were living in Boston, I didn't mind if people knew that I was in the Program. I didn't need to explain to anybody why I was there, because my friends all knew what I was like when I drank. But in New York and Connecticut, nobody had ever seen me drunk. When my new friends asked me why I didn't drink, I said that I had been a little wild when I was younger and that I just liked my life better without drinking. Most people were fine with that explanation, and several friends empathized: they, too, had been wild in their youth, they explained, also binge drinkers who occasionally suffered blackouts, but that they had grown out of that behavior. "When I became a mom, I changed," a friend told me. "I could never party now the way I used to. I just have a glass of wine or two with my husband at dinner. Maybe a couple drinks at a party. That's it."

I didn't drink for another five years, but during those years, I started entertaining the fantasy that I, too, might have been able to become a social drinker, had I given myself time to mature. The thing that kept me from helping myself to a nip of my husband's vodka or ordering a drink when I was out with friends was the Program. I had been Programmed not to drink. In the Program, they say that "the first drink gets you drunk," and I had become terrified of taking that first drink. After that first drink, all bets were off. If I had even one glass of wine, I feared I would be compelled to have another and another until I awoke from a blackout, behind prison bars. My children would be in the custody of child protective services, where they would remain until my husband's body could be located. I am not exaggerating; that is how fearful of alcohol I had become. To choose to take a drink was to choose to destroy my life and my family.

That hot day at the island resort, however, I hadn't chosen to take a drink. I had asked for a fruit punch. *They had misunderstood.* On another day, in another place, if I had been rested and well-fed, if I wasn't enraged at my husband and fed up with my children, if I wasn't filled with self-loathing over the botched flight arrangements, I would have asked the waiter what was in the drink as soon as I saw its color. That day, I didn't. I hadn't asked for a drink, but here I was sipping one.

It was an accident.

After my second sip or third sip, I decided to turn it into an experiment.

An alcoholic would be compelled to order another drink and then another and another after that first rum punch. I left the drink half-full on the reception desk when the valet led us to our rooms, and I didn't look back. When he showed us the complimentary bottle of island rum that sat on top of the refrigerator, I barely glanced at it. I didn't feel like having that rum. An alcoholic would have opened the bottle and started chugging its contents the moment her husband turned his back. I suggested we all go to the beach for a swim, and for the rest of that day, I swam and strolled on the beach in a sort of daze, just filled with a sense of euphoric wonder. It seemed that I could have one drink, after all. I could stop drinking once I started. Perhaps I was not an alcoholic. Later that night, I tested my hypothesis by pouring a slug full of the free rum into my coke and sipping it before we headed down to dinner. I didn't want another drink at dinner. It was official. I was not an alcoholic. It felt, then, that I had been living some sort of stagnant half-life for years, but now I was whole again. Suddenly everything was clear: I had been enslaved by the tyranny of the cultish Program, but now I was free.

I didn't tell my husband about my discovery until we returned to Connecticut. It had been fourteen years since he had seen me drunk. At first, he was skeptical, but after spending a few nights with the new me, I had him convinced that I could drink again. For some people, alcohol lessens their inhibitions and makes their sex lives more interesting. I'm rather uninhibited naturally—my baseline is just a hair above exhibitionist—and when I drink, I'm what a former boyfriend once called "a bit of a handful, but lots of fun," so who could blame my husband for overlooking, with me, the signs that I was not really in control of my drinking at all. We started having all that fun with my being a handful again. Plus, he was away a lot of the time, so he didn't see me drunk on a regular basis, and I was careful that the kids and my friends didn't either. I would pour a glass of wine while cooking dinner and would only refill it when the kids were out of the room. That way it looked like I was drinking the same glass of wine all night, when, in truth, I often consumed more, usually after they went to bed. When I was out with friends, I never had more than two glasses of wine. I had to drive home, and I wasn't going to drive while intoxicated. That's what alcoholics did. When I arrived home, checked on my sleeping children, and sent the babysitter on her way, I would enjoy a bottle on my own.

Yes, I had my moments of doubt, but they were easy to dispel. I hadn't eaten enough. Everybody was drunk at that party. I'm a grown-up! Grown-ups sometimes get drunk! Now I knew the truth: the perspective of the Program was totally warped. I had been like a dependent child when I had been in the Program. I had been brainwashed into thinking that I had a drinking problem, when, really, I assured myself, I drank like most other adults. In the Program, people talked about how, once you had a "slip," you would lose everything you had gained in your sobriety. It would be a fast, downhill slide straight to the gutter. But I had my first book published during those few years I returned to drinking. I went on a book tour and attended book parties, very careful to stick to the two- or three-glass maximum while out. My life got better when I drank; that was proof enough that I wasn't an alcoholic.

Right? I would ask myself, as I poured the last drops of a bottle into my glass, all alone in the dark with my dogs. Right? I asked as I staggered to the fridge for a fresh bottle.

I won't bore you with how I stopped drinking and returned to the Program again. But I will say that my lifelong desire to be liked, my need for approval, my deeply ingrained need to be seen as "nice," worked in my favor when it came to overcoming my alcoholism.

After I published a novel about an alcoholic in denial, I did lots of interviews that included discussions about my own alcoholism. People began asking my advice about their friends or family members who were problem drinkers, and again and again they told me the same thing: their alcoholic family member or loved one was Such A Nice Person when sober, but when they drank they became unbearably mean or messy or embarrassing. The problem was that it seemed impossible to confront the drinker the next day, because they'd become So Very Nice again.

Many people naturally assume that the mean things a drunk says reflect the way the drunk really feels. The theory is that alcohol lowers inhibitions and the person no longer tries to hide their true feelings. This isn't entirely accurate. Drunks, in my experience, may declare hatred for a person who has triggered their anger in that moment, or may pronounce undying love for a person they've just met, but those aren't true feelings. I'm no professional, I can only extrapolate from my own experience, but the only thing that was entirely inhibited when I drank was my self-loathing. After those first two or three drinks, I was funnier, smarter, prettier than I had been an hour earlier. And then I had an uncontrollable compulsion to keep fueling that newfound self-love with what had provided it in the first place—booze.

The alcoholics in my family—and there have been many,

generation after generation—drink like I did. We skip the years of normal drinking that some alcoholics have before they get out of control. We launch headlong into blackout drinking right off the bat. We have to do a lot of bullshitting the next day, taking care to be extra nice after a bad drinking episode. We work hard to cover our tracks, though we often don't even know where the tracks are.

I'd seen drunken behavior from a very early age and, sure, it's sometimes funny, but it's usually not very funny for long. This, I now understand, has been a blessing.

We hadn't been together more than a year when Denis told me, after a bad night, that when I got drunk, I reminded him of a person we knew who was a particularly embarrassing alcoholic. I was instantly aware that the riotously funny and highly intellectual supermodel I'd seen in the bathroom mirror after my second or third drink bore no resemblance to the insufferable mess everybody else saw staggering around the rest of the night. I think that was the first time I tried to stop drinking for good.

You who are non-alcoholics probably enjoy a drink or two on a daily or weekly basis. You might occasionally overindulge on weekends. We alcoholics try, every time we pick up a drink, to be like you. Every single time we drink, we believe: this time will be different. Yes, it's insane, but that's what we think. And no matter how much we insist that we don't have a problem, that we just didn't eat enough that night, that we were no worse than anybody else at that party—there is a very desperate and terrified inner voice asking, right? Am I right? We know the answer. We know there's a problem. But the solution—not drinking—seems unfathomable.

When I first started going to meetings regularly, at age twenty-four, another person in the Program asked me a question that would turn out to be the most important thing anyone could have said to me about my drinking: "All those things that you're so ashamed of, all those embarrassing or even illegal things you did—would you have done them without drinking?" This guy was a stranger—I hadn't told him anything about myself—yet somehow, he knew everything about why I was there. Of course, the answer to his question was no. Only a sociopath would behave the way I did when I drank. But that question lit my first spark of hope. Maybe I wasn't fundamentally an asshole or a lunatic. Maybe I was just an alcoholic. I was never going to be perfect, he went on to say, I would always have flaws—maybe I'd turn out to be an asshole or a lunatic without alcohol—the only thing he could say with absolute certainty was that if I didn't drink, I wouldn't get drunk.

When I returned to the Program after my slip, a friend said more or less the same thing. My biggest problem was not my personality, it was booze; I needed to stop drinking. I was also reminded, by listening to my fellow drunks, that a time would come when I would rarely, if ever, have a desire for alcohol. But I had to stop drinking first.

And I did.

And they were right.

OLD DOG, NEW TRICKS

I was almost at my banjo lesson when I realized that I'd forgotten my written homework again. My assignment was to write out all the notes of the major scales, which I'd done the night before. But I forgot to bring it, and if I went back to get it, I'd be late. I arrived at my lesson full of regret and shame, and as anticipated, my teacher, Roger, was annoyed when I told him. He didn't believe I did the homework. When I stammered that I did, I really did, even I didn't believe me.

"Have you practiced?" he asked.

Had I ever! This would erase the homework fiasco from Roger's mind. My left hand delicately supported the neck of the banjo, and I positioned my right hand over the strings on the banjo's drum, my pinkie and ring finger supporting my hand, just as Roger had taught me. We'd been working on a song that I'd practiced all week, and just the day before, I could play it quite fast. Now I was a nervous wreck and couldn't remember the first chord.

Roger reminded me.

I started to play the song, but I was stiff and robotic; my fingers couldn't seem to find the strings.

"Sing along with it," Roger said, as he always did. "It helps if you sing along."

"OLD SU-SANNA, oh, don't you cry for me," I crooned, my foot tapping the beat on the floor.

"Wait, wait, whoa! It's not 'Old Susanna.' It's 'Oh! Susanna.'" Roger said.

"Are you sure?" I asked. How could it be Oh! Susanna? I learned this song in nursery school, and it was always Old Susanna."

Roger closed his eyes in what I assumed was a silent prayer for patience.

"Yes," he finally said. "OH! SUSANNA!"

I'm not reminiscing about a time in my youth when I tried to learn a musical instrument. I was in my forties, but I always felt like I was about twelve during my banjo lessons with Roger, and not just because Roger was eighty-four. It turns out that learning new skills in midlife is a great way to feel young again.

Since I turned forty, I have learned, among other things, how to play tennis, drive an ambulance, design a website, write a bestselling book, and deftly back a truck pulling a horse trailer into a parking space. I've studied a form of animal training that focuses on operant conditioning and positive reinforcement, and now my unhinged rescue dog has earned every trick title offered by the AKC, and I have a pony who can dance. I learned how to perform CPR, the

Heimlich maneuver, and various other lifesaving techniques, which allowed me to become a certified emergency medical technician. What else, what else? OH, decoupage! Plant care. In short, I'm a hobbyist.

When I started taking banjo lessons, I was working on a book about a family that played bluegrass music. I began listening to a lot of bluegrass music, and became obsessed with the banjo, an instrument I'd heard all my life but never fully appreciated. I don't think there's a happier-sounding instrument than the banjo. You can play anything on it—play sad songs if you feel like it, but it seems like a waste. Wherever there's a banjo, you're likely to find a fiddle, which is much more suited to sad music. Anyway, while I was writing this novel and listening to bluegrass, I learned about the African origins of the banjo and became determined to learn how to play it.

But by my second month of banjo lessons, I was becoming increasingly aware of the limitations of my learning capacity and began to think the whole thing was hopeless. I didn't know it then, but I was at Stage Two of something I found on the internet called the Conscious Competence Learning Matrix. This matrix outlines a model created in the 1970s at the Gordon Training International organization in Solana Beach, California. It was originally known as the Four Stages of Learning and is best understood in chart form (see the next page).

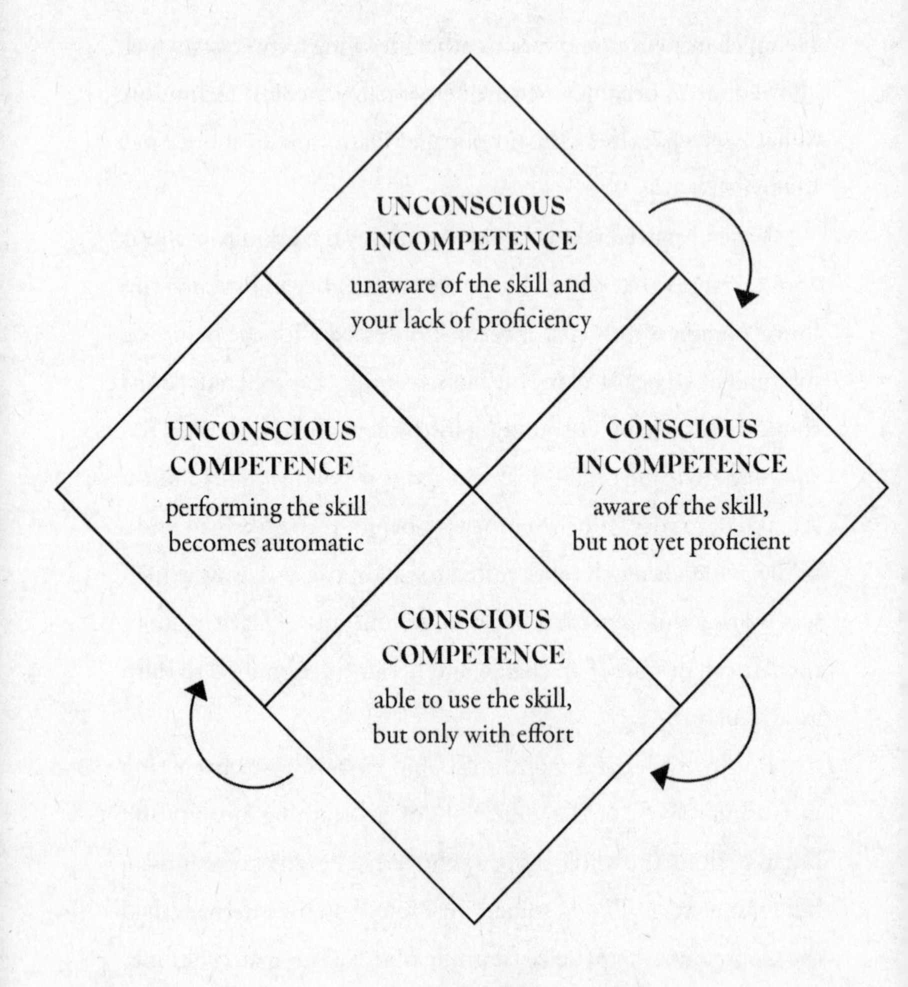

Credited to:
Gordon Training International
by its employee Noel Burch in the 1970s

Adapted from "Competence Hierarchy adapted from Noel Burch by Igor Kokcharov" created by Igor Kokcharov, June 25, 2015. Wikipedia. https://commons.wikimedia.org/wiki File:Competence_Hierarchy_adapted_from_Noel_Burch_by_Igor_Kokcharov.jpg

Just a month prior, I was at Stage One: Unconscious Incompetence. Stage One is a very happy place. A child of two is not embarrassed that she's a lousy dancer because she has no idea she's lousy. She dances, people clap—she's happy.

After my first banjo lesson, I was happy too. I'd been lucky enough to find out that a bluegrass legend named Roger Sprung lived only a few miles from my house. I bought a cheap banjo, Roger taught me how to play a few chords, and my enthusiasm knew no bounds. I didn't know that I was then in a textbook Stage One: Unconsciously Incompetent. I thought, because I knew three chords that could be played with some simple tunes, that I was somewhat competent.

I took the banjo home and played it for Denis. Denis plays the guitar, so he watched with rapt attention as I played for him. When I finished, he said, "Oh. Okay. What's the song called?"

I had just played him the C scale. Do-re-mi-fa-sol-la-ti-do. When I told him that's what I'd played, he said there was nothing in the ten minutes of my fumbling, thumping, humming, and plucking at the strings that sounded like any musical scale. Which thrust me squarely into Stage Two: Conscious Incompetence. According to learning experts, this is when most people quit. Fortunately, I have a lot of experience with Stage Two. In fact, I'm Consciously Incompetent at cooking, handwriting, organizing, cleaning—pretty much everything useful in daily life, so I wasn't ready to quit banjo. I was just more aware of how difficult it was going to be to learn.

And this is what is different about the way I approach learning now, in my prime, compared with the way I approached it in my youth.

When I was a kid, I took piano lessons. My goal was to play and sing in a concert, in front of thousands, just like Joni Mitchell. I had my own learning matrix, which went something like this:

> Stage One: Conscious Awe. Admiration of a cool skill possessed by other (usually famous) individuals.
>
> Stage Two: Unconscious Insanity. Delusional state in which I am certain that, with a little training and practice, I will soon master said skill and learn to deal with the adoration of strangers and the bitter envy of my friends.
>
> Stage Three: Conscious Mounting Shame. Awareness of personal deficits in the areas of memory, intellect, and coordination.
>
> Stage Four: Unconscious Quitting. A decision is made to "take a little time off" from learning the new skill. Revert to hobbies already mastered like reading and watching television.

Today, despite the frustration and embarrassment, I'm usually able to see value in the process of learning new skills without worrying too much about the outcome. Learning new tricks is very therapeutic for this old dog. When I become stuck in my writing, I can pick up my banjo and everything is removed from my mind but the strings and my fingers and how to get them to work together. And in trying to learn one thing, I learn countless things I hadn't anticipated.

For example, do you know the difference between a major chord and a minor chord? I do. The major chords are the happy chords; the minor chords are sad. Music is logical; it's formed of patterns and sequences that are mathematical and precise. I learned all this while I was still in the Unconscious Incompetence stage.

When I started my lessons, I wanted to be able to pick up the banjo any old time and blow people's minds. I imagined coming across a couple of bluegrass buskers on a street corner. The banjo player, noticing that my learned eye was trained on his rolls and vamps, would offer up his instrument and the fiddler and I would play "Orange Blossom Special," and then we'd improvise for fun.

I used to think that bluegrass music, like jazz, was highly improvisational. What I learned is that in order to improvise—to make up one's own rules—one must first learn the rules. This goes for pretty much everything. There's no skipping steps on the competency scale, but there's no shame in hanging out on one of the steps, either. I'm rather enjoying my time on the Conscious Incompetence step of learning the banjo, and that's a good thing because I've been here for years. Once we moved, I was no longer close enough for my lessons with Roger, but I still pick up my old banjo now and then and my C scale is perfection.

LOVE MEANS NOTHING (IN TENNIS)

When our son, Jack, was about thirteen, I watched him taking a tennis lesson one day and thought, *Now that looks like a good workout.* I assumed that since I was forty, I'd never be good enough to play any real tennis, but chasing the ball around the court for an hour or two a week might help me tone up a bit.

I began taking lessons from Jack's instructor; he was the local pro—a preppy, middle-aged man named Spenser. Amazingly, after a couple of months of being able to return balls that Spenser hit softly into my racket, I was able to occasionally hit balls that he lobbed high into the air or torpedoed right at my feet. Eventually, he told me I needed to practice by playing with others. He said that he'd fix me up with people who played at my level.

My playing peers often arrived at the courts in cars with handicapped parking access signs dangling from their rearview mirrors. One actually used a walker. She pushed the walker across the pavement, parked it at the water cooler, then she shuffled over to the court next to her partner—a stooped woman who appeared to have an advanced stage of osteoporosis. My own partner was closer to my age, but she had braces on both knees and one elbow. I'd become somewhat adept at getting the ball over the net and felt that I needed to be gentle with the two old dears on the other side of the court. As it happened, my opponents had been playing tennis since they were children, sometime during the Depression Era. They couldn't move but if I hit the ball anywhere near them—which I did a lot, as I wasn't great at placing my shots—they'd return it and place it exactly where I was not. They were unbeatable.

I began playing in a doubles group that consisted of women closer to my age. They weren't great tennis players, they weren't even good, but they were all better than me. When it came time to partner up, I'd gaze off into the horizon and pretend that I was taking in the beauty of the nearby dumpsters so as not to go through the agony of watching the others try to shove their way over to the opposite side of the net from where I stood. The good sport who was left on my side usually bravely chirped something like, "Okay, looks like Ann and I'll be partners!" Then she braced herself for the inevitable battering. Tennis is a gentleman's sport, thank God, so I could trust that my partner wouldn't whack me on the back of the head with her racket when I hit a volley right into the net, again. Instead, she usually began the game with encouraging words like, "Nice try!" or "That's a tough shot!" (This through gritted teeth, after the ball landed squarely in my racket and, in a fit of astonished excitement, I sent it soaring over our opponents, over the baseline, over the fence, and into the parking lot.)

Denis was happy to play with me as long as we didn't have to play by the rules. As he repeatedly explained, playing by the rules placed him at an unfair disadvantage because he didn't know the rules, and he didn't know how to serve. Instead of learning the rules, he wanted to play a variation of tennis he had invented with another actor while on location in a tropical country. Their game involved no serving and a complicated but curiously malleable set of regulations that often appeared, to me, to change midgame and almost always to Denis's advantage. This caused some heated courtside squabbles. I'm ashamed to admit that one year we spent several days of a family vacation not speaking to each other after a game of "Denis Tennis" that I had lost "unfairly" (I repeatedly hissed at our children), until finally Jack and Devin had to intervene and coerce a truce between us.

I kept taking lessons. I wanted to learn the ins and outs of tennis—the real tennis, the Queen's tennis—because unlike Denis, I was a good sport. Unlike him, I believed in playing by the rules. This was a time when it had become a habit of mine to mentally pit my character against Denis's in this way, and I was always the winner. Later, I would learn, to my complete amazement, that he was also silently comparing and contrasting our personalities, and for some reason he thought he was the superior person. So, yes, our marriage was going through a bit of a rough patch, and I believe, in retrospect, tennis filled a void for me. It was my new love.

I played whenever I could. I continued working on my stroke because I believed if I improved enough, I'd be able to beat Denis at his own game (which was impossible because of the whole rule-changing thing). I had a bit of a breakthrough while taking lessons from a Russian named Ivan. One day, we were hitting the ball back and forth, and he had me doing this drill where you hit the ball cross-court, then hit the ball straight ahead, then run over to the backhand court, hit the ball cross-court, then straight ahead, etc. It was quite fun, but I was often hitting shots into the net. I believed this was because I wasn't swinging properly. Ivan said, "You're a little stiff." I said that yes, my shoulders were a little stiff; I'd been sitting at the computer all morning. Ivan said, "No, your legs. When you run, you don't bend your knees."

"I don't bend my knees when I run?"

"No," said Ivan. And then I was treated to a demonstration of the way I run. Imagine a person running who has no knees. In order to create momentum, they tilt their upper body forward and then their ramrod straight limbs sort of stagger along behind them, Frankenstein's monster style. When I saw Ivan do this, I instantly realized that: (a) I was watching the funniest thing I'd seen since Don Knotts died; and (b) he was, in fact, not trying to be funny but was doing a dead-on impersonation of me running. It turns out that for the past five years of trying to learn tennis, I had not bent my knees. Not while swinging. Not while running. I don't know why—the knees bend.

I'd been playing for a couple of years when Denis and I went to a place in the Bahamas during the kids' spring break. I decided to book a lesson with an amazing pro named Louis. Denis took a few lessons with Louis too. We both tried to guess his age. He could have been fifty, he could have been eighty. He was very fit for whatever his age was, and very formal and old-fashioned on the courts—always wearing a white polo shirt tucked into crisp white shorts. He had perfect posture and exuded calm, assertive energy at all times. *The Dog Whisperer* was a popular show at that time, and although I didn't love Cesar Millan's training methods, I was interested in what he said about the psychological state that one must achieve in order to effectively communicate with people and animals. If one is able to exude calm, assertive energy, he promised, it was possible to bring out the same energy in others.

When I had my first lesson with Louis, he told me that my stranglehold on the grip and fierce swatting at the ball would result in elbow injuries. He also told me that I had excessive "New York" energy, and that I should try to let go of that and remember that I am in his native Bahamas, where people don't feel such a sense of urgency all the time.

The second day there, I went down to the courts for my lesson with Louis, but Louis was booked and instead, I had a lesson with his son, Kevin. Kevin was gorgeous. He eschewed the formal whites worn by his father and wore cool tennis clothes and sneakers. His dreadlocks were pulled back in a loose ponytail. He looked like he spent most of his off-court time in the gym or modeling. I was at an age where I felt I could crush on younger guys and it was harmless—Kevin was not much older than my son, after all. But although Kevin was calm and polite and friendly, he brought out what Cesar Millan would call "excited energy" in me. I was like those nutty Pomeranians that race around yapping at nothing. I was giggling and whacking the ball and cackling and swatting at the ball, and when Kevin leapt the net to my side of the court to readjust my grip, I had a hard time breathing properly. Louis finished his lesson and frowned at us from the sidelines. When my hour was up, Louis said that he would give me my lesson the next day.

The next day, I arrived at the court, running and bellowing apologies for being a few minutes late. Louis stood calmly and then asked, quietly, if I was ready to begin. This made me answer, quietly, that I was. And then he gave me the best tennis lesson I've ever had, laced with all sorts of philosophy and psychology that made the sport seem like some sort of Zen guide to enlightened living. Here's an example: I tend to hit the ball hard, but my follow-through sucks. Louis explained that anybody can hit a ball hard, but the follow-through gives the ball direction. Then he said, "Any woman can have children, but it's not where the children start, it's where they end up that is important. Anybody can start a business, but without direction, without follow-through, it will go nowhere."

He told me that he can see that I'm a little competitive, and while being competitive is fine, in my case, it's getting in my way, because I don't have the basic tools—the skills required to focus all this competitive energy. And I have to relax. The tension, the tension, the tension, he said. He had me hold the racket with just my thumb and forefinger and hit the ball several times like that, just to show me that I didn't need to smash at each ball as if it were the last ball I'd ever hit. The ball skimmed over the net when I hit it this way. Then he let me hold it the proper way and we just hit balls, back and forth. I focused on the smooth arc of my swing, not on where

I wanted to smash the ball. I watched the ball, and when I met it with my racket, I followed through. Again and again and again.

It's not where the ball, or the child or the book or the marriage or the job, starts. It's where it ends up that's important. And in fact, tennis eventually helped us sort out some of the problems in our marriage, just a few years later.

Though Denis and I had found tennis somewhat late in life, we had found each other quite early. When we moved in together, I was twenty, he twenty-five. We were too young and inexperienced then to know that people don't change who they are, only how they play and work with others. Our basic problem was, and is, that we are almost identical—in looks, attitudes, and psychological makeup. Two Leos who love children and animals and are intensely emotional and highly sensitive and competitive with everybody, but especially with each other.

When the children came along, we got caught up in the tallying of efforts, the scorekeeping of who was doing more for the marriage and family and who was being self-serving, unloving, and disapproving. Somewhere along the line we had entered a long-running silent competition in which we weren't partners—we were opponents. We didn't bicker often, but when we fought, we raged.

We began to see a marriage counselor, who, among other things, suggested that we have a regular date night. Our apathy was such that our date night was our marriage-counseling night.

We went to our weekly counseling session and afterward, we sometimes went to a movie. One of the movies we saw was *March of the Penguins*. This movie moved us to tears because whatever battles raged between us, however ugly the other often appeared to be, we had these two very delicate fledglings that needed to be protected and carried along carefully, so carefully, because is anything more fragile than a preteen girl or a growing, unsure boy?

These great children were the reason we were in counseling, the reason we were trying to keep the family egg whole. So we worked hard at playing nice. We had regular family nights and took family vacations. And on occasion we tried to play tennis together. Despite all of this, the marriage continued to flounder, and the time came when we met in our marriage counselor's office and I said, "I think it's over."

"That's it," Denis agreed.

When we left, it felt as if we were floating, we were so calm. We had stormed out of those doors and stomped down those steps in such rages before, but now Denis held the door for me, and I thanked him. When we got to the street, it was snowing. I had boots with heels, and the sidewalks were icy. I couldn't walk on the icy sidewalks with those heels, so I asked if I could hold his arm, if he could walk me home.

"Sure," he said. He didn't care.

Neither did I. I just needed something to hold on to so I wouldn't slip and fall. I clung to his arm, and we bent our bodies into the wind.

"The thing is," he said as we walked, "I'm tired and hungry."

"Let's get something to eat," I said.

We went to the restaurant across from our building, a little neighborhood place where the waiters know our names and the chef knows how we like our burgers. We sat in a booth in the back. Denis ordered soup.

It was all over, there was nothing to lose, so I decided to serve up my final grievances, the things I felt he needed to know to fully understand that he was the cause of our marriage's untimely end. I reminded him, in a resigned tone, of the time he did this, the time he did that.

These were the wretched rags of resentment so bitter and old, so petty, that I had been too ashamed even to mention them in therapy, so now I balled them up and tossed them onto Denis's court.

Denis just ate his soup. When he was finished, he wiped his chin with his napkin. We were both so calm, it was as if the island of Manhattan had been gassed with some kind of Valium vapor.

I guess there was no emotion left, it was all over, and we both experienced this finality as a surprising relief. We were like the penguin couple in *March of the Penguins* that accidentally dropped and broke their egg. They looked at the egg for a time, and then they parted ways, because penguins don't mate for life. They court each other, commit each other's voice to memory, produce an egg, devote themselves to its care, and when it dies, or matures, the parents part company. This was how we had come to view our marriage, as a penguin marriage, a partnership devoted to raising children. We had hoped to stick it out until they left the nest, but now it looked as if that would be impossible. So we were just having a last look.

Denis carefully refolded his napkin, and then said: "I'm sorry. If I could change those things I would, but I can't. They're in the past. But, I'm sorry."

I had expected him to cry foul, to react the way he did when I said a questionable tennis shot of his was out. But he just said he was sorry. And I believed him. He had no reason to make up that kind of thing now. His calm admission inspired me to exhale my own litany of regrets and apologies. In the movies, this would have been the moment we leapt into each other's embrace, but in real life, we ordered more food. We called the children in the apartment to see if they wanted to go to a movie. That night Denis didn't stay in a hotel; he stayed home. The next day we all drove to the country. The family, after all that mad jostling, somehow had remained intact.

What happened that night? I'm not sure I know. But I forgot to mention that our shrink never believed us when we complained about the hopelessness of our marriage, and he didn't believe us when we said it was over. During the months of sessions, he kept catching us doing this thing in the middle of all the verbal sparring. I would attack Denis, he would berate me, but whenever the therapist said anything in the least bit negative about either of us, we would jump to the other's defense. The therapist would say something like, "Ann, it sounds like your negativity can sometimes create a problem in situations like that," and Denis would say, "Ann's not negative. I don't know anybody who would describe her that way." Or the shrink would suggest that a joke Denis had just made at my expense had hurt me deeply, because I'd grabbed a tissue and pressed it to my eyes. But then he'd see that the tears were streaming from my eyes because I was laughing so hard at what Denis had just said (I'm one of those people who is unable to fully laugh without crying). The shrink kept pointing these things out and we'd say, "But all couples stick up for each other." Our shrink insisted that, in his experience, they don't. We thought he was stringing us along for the money.

The night that we declared the marriage over, we said goodbye to the therapist—we thought—for good. We thanked him for trying. When we showed up the next week, he was expecting us.

So, things got better. We went to the shrink. We went to our movies. We worked at treating each other more fairly. And we started playing a lot of tennis, just the two of us, whenever we could. Only now, we played by the rules.

Though I had many lessons under my belt, Denis is the better athlete, so almost immediately we played on more or less the same level. We improved every game. We stopped cheating. (Yes, I admit, we both used to call questionable shots out when we were backed into a corner, and we used to fudge the score if we could, both of us.) We were still ultracompetitive, but now we were becoming intensely proud when the other hit an amazing shot, and we didn't hate the winner when we lost. We still played to win, but now we could feel joy for the other. We wanted to improve, and now we wanted, were actually thrilled, to see the other get better, too.

Denis and I had a last tennis match before we packed up our son and drove him to college. We had spent that summer knowing we were at the beginning of the end of something that we didn't want to end. On the court, that last morning of our vacation, we had each won a set and it was 5–5 in the final set. We had reserved the court for only an hour, though, and the hour was almost up. There were other players waiting. This would have to be the final game of the match, but the games had been so hard-won that neither of us could bear to lose.

Denis was serving in this deciding game. He served carefully and didn't try to ace it past me as he typically did. Too risky. I didn't take advantage by slamming my return into his backhand court. What if it went out? The match would be over.

I hit the ball into his court, and he hit it back into mine. I placed the ball in his court carefully, *so carefully*, and he placed it back in mine. We rallied, not with the adrenaline-pumping determination to win at all costs, but with the patience and control that came with not wanting it to be over: not the summer, not our son's childhood, not this game, ever.

Back and forth we sent the ball. And it occurred to me there was some sort of grace in my husband's form, and I felt it in mine, too, as we both worked to keep the game alive just a little longer, by trying to find each other's sweet spot, by playing, for once, to the other's advantage.

THE FIXER

Many writers have funny stories about family members' reactions to their work. In her memoir, *Cool, Calm and Contentious*, award-winning television writer Merrill Markoe recounts the first time she showed her mother something she'd written. Merrill, like all fledgling writers, was insecure about her talents. She asked her mother what she thought about what Merrill had written. Her mother replied, sadly, "Well, I don't particularly care for it, but I pray I'm wrong."

I met a writer at a party who told me his mother claimed to love his novel. She even wrote a nice review about it on Amazon, but she only gave him four out of five stars. When he asked why she didn't give him five, she said, "Well, it's a wonderful story, dear, but it's not perfect."

My mother has always been a champion of my career as a writer and has celebrated my work with just a few exceptions. In my first book, which was a memoir, Mom felt a certain chapter portrayed her in an unfavorable light. Then there was my novel, *The Good*

House, which is told from the point of view of a sixty-year-old woman named Hildy who lives on the North Shore of Boston. And who may or may not have a drinking problem. Hildy has, at times, strained relationships with her grown daughters. My mother, like Hildy, lives on the North Shore of Boston, and she, my sister, and I have had some disputes, like most families.

And that's where any similarity between Hildy and my mother ends. Hildy is a lifelong New Englander, a rough-around-the edges townie whose ancestor was one of the witches hanged in Salem. She's an excellent observer when it comes to people. In fact, her intuitive skills have not only helped her business as a real-estate broker, many people believe she's a psychic because she has an uncanny ability to "read" another person, immediately assess their inner nature—and relate to them accordingly. My mother is a voracious reader of books, but she can't read a person or a room to save her life. She means well, but she's the type of person who, upon entering a dark alley filled with rivaling gang members, might break the ice by asking who's been to Symphony Hall since it was renovated. Nobody? Well, they must go, it's divine.

When I delivered the first draft of *The Good House* to my editor, my mother asked to read it. I believe I sent it to her on a Friday. That Sunday evening, she left a sad, quiet message on our answering machine, saying: "Thank you for sending the book. I read it over the weekend. Congratulations. What an accomplishment . . . writing a book." The message faded out with words that might have included "goodbye." It was obvious that she'd had to heavily self-medicate just to make that call.

I phoned her the next day, and she sounded a little brighter. I asked her what she really thought about the book and, after pausing for what felt like an hour but was probably less than a minute, she said, "I'm just worried about . . . I mean, who do you think the reading audience would be for something . . . like this?"

I was breaking out in a sweat. I knew it. The book was unreadable. A disaster. "I guess, adults. Hopefully a lot of adults," I finally said, heart racing.

She maintained her sympathetic tone. "You know, Ann, I just don't think it would be fair for me to weigh in on this. You're too far along in the process to change anything now."

I told her that it wasn't too late to change anything. It was just a first draft. My editor would have lots of notes, what did she think I should change? How could I make it better?

"No," she insisted, "it just wouldn't be fair. I read different kinds of books. My book group reads very serious literature. In fact, we just read the new Jeffrey Eugenides. So, I don't think I'm the right person to weigh in on your book, especially at this late stage. But I'm so proud of you, really."

I don't remember the entire conversation, but at some point, in response to my prodding, she did say she was worried about reactions from readers. They might not understand that it's fiction, and because it's about an alcoholic, they might make embarrassing inferences about me as the author, was the gist.

I'll pause here to explain that my mother is heavily into gists, and I believe this might tie into my problems with trying too hard to be nice and my excessive worrying about what others think about me. I have many friends whose mothers are in the habit of saying openly hostile things to them, and that's terrible. My mother's not like that. She will compliment me if she likes something, but if she doesn't like a new haircut, or outfit, she'll say, in a sometimes confused tone, "You've changed your hair." Or "Isn't that an interesting outfit?" If I were to shave my head and cover it with tattoos of my dog, I believe my mother would say, "You've changed your hair." What's left unsaid is *everything*.

To be fair, my mother is very polite and believes that if one can't say something nice—it's best to say nothing at all. But, having been raised in a family that favors this cryptic communication style, I often imagine deeply loaded subtexts in lighthearted conversations with others.

"After you," somebody will say as we approach a checkout line at the supermarket. I'm slightly in front of the person, but because they said "after you," I assume I've just cut in front. "Oh my God, I'm so sorry, were you first? Please go," I'll say, adding a few "I'm so sorrys." The person tells me that no, I had been first. But then why did they ask? I'll press. Now the checkout clerk, and everybody else in line, is exasperated.

"What did you have for lunch?" my tennis partner asks. My hand flies to my mouth and I mumble, "There's lettuce all over my teeth, right?" In fact, she just wanted to know if I ate before the match.

Would I prefer that my mother, like Mrs. Markoe, had said, "I don't happen to care for it, but I pray I'm wrong"? I don't think so, but at least I'd know what she thought—she didn't care for it. My mother said that she couldn't tell me what she thought about my writing because it wouldn't be fair *to me*. The gist as I interpreted it: She was protecting me. The truth was too horrible to be spoken aloud.

Then I remembered how my mother had framed her response to a scene that included her in my first book—the memoir. She hadn't said, "I'm worried about what people will think of me when they read what you wrote about me." She had said, "I don't mind what you wrote. I'm worried about the readers' reactions. I think readers will be turned off by that scene."

When I asked her to be specific about what might turn them off, she said, "Well, they're going to think you're terribly ungrateful, for one." *She* didn't think I was ungrateful, but she was worried that "the readers" might. She wanted to protect me.

After our conversation about the memoir, Mom decided to edit the problematic chapter, which took place in a London hospital where I was a patient. She added a few extraneous scenes about things that happened to her while I was in the hospital, rewrote almost every word of dialogue, and sent it back to me. Now Mom spoke and behaved like Julie Andrews in *Mary Poppins*. I was a grown-up version of the little girl in the movie *The Bad Seed*, only more grateful. I told her I enjoyed her short story, but I was supposed to write my own book. Ultimately, I cut out most of the stuff she didn't like, and it all worked out in the end because all those potentially turned-off readers, from what I can make out in royalty statements, never even bought the book.

Now we were discussing my attempt to write a novel that she thought would turn people off. *Well, you wrote a book* was Mom's attitude for the entire year leading up to the book's publication. When it was published, it landed on the *New York Times* bestseller list and was immediately optioned for a film. Offers for foreign sales were rolling in, and during that very heady time, my mother called me one day to tell me that she was very proud of me and the book. She had decided to listen to the audio version, which was narrated by the talented actress Mary Beth Hurt. Mom was astounded at what an amazing job she'd done with it. She loved it and asked if I'd listened to it. I have a hard time listening to audio versions of my novels. I had listened to some of it and knew Mary Beth had done a stellar job. I said so to my mother.

"Oh, but you have to listen to the whole thing," Mom said. "You have no idea how good it is. It's great."

I said, "I wrote the book, so I do have a sense of it."

"No," she insisted. "Mary Beth Hurt really adds something. I'm only about halfway through, but I can't stop listening."

I had book events in the Boston area soon after that, and almost immediately after I'd arrived at my mother's house, where I was staying, she brought up Mary Beth Hurt's narration again.

"Have you listened to it yet?" she said.

I was in that mixed emotional state that comes from all the interviews and events surrounding a book launch. I'd had some well-attended events and some sparsely attended events. I'd had some great reviews and some mixed reviews. I was exhausted. So, I know I was short with Mom when I said, through clenched teeth, that, no, I hadn't listened to the book, but I know Mary Beth Hurt fixed it for me, because she'd already told me so.

"But there's something wrong with the ending," Mom said. "I think the audio version left out the last chapter or something. It just ends."

I like novels that don't conclude with everything neatly tied up—I like slightly open endings. I'd decided to leave a little to the reader's imagination regarding the fate of the main characters at the end of that novel. Some readers, according to Goodreads and Amazon reviews, didn't appreciate this decision.

"I get it. You hate the ending. You're not alone," I said to my mother. "Other people don't like the way it ends, either."

"No," she insisted. "Listen to it, I don't think it ends at the right place." And she thrust her headphones at me. "Listen!"

"Jesus, Mom, I KNOW!" I snapped, very bad seed–like. "You hate the way it ends. You're not alone. SORRY I DIDN'T WRAP IT UP LIKE A FUCKING FAIRY TALE FOR YOU."

My mother just gazed at me for a moment. Then she placed her phone on the coffee table and said, with a Julie Andrews calm, "It's cued up to the last paragraph of the book."

I put the earphones on and listened. My poor mother—she had no idea what she was talking about. It wasn't cued up to the last paragraph of the book. I was listening to something that happened several chapters before the ending. I was about to explain this to her when, to my great surprise, the recording stopped at the end of that paragraph, and Mary Beth Hurt's narration was replaced by the audiobook's closing credits. I pressed rewind, then fast-forward, but it ended at the same place. Then I downloaded another audio version on my own phone, and it too came to an abrupt stop seventy-five pages before the end of the novel. Now those online reviews made more sense. The audiobook did stop abruptly; it wasn't just open-ended—it had no ending. The producers of the audiobook had somehow not included the last chapters of the book. Audible and other audiobook platforms sold unfinished copies of my book for weeks. Nobody at my publisher, nor I, had any idea.

My mother was the one who found the snafu. She saved my audiobook. The final chapters were added the next day.

RED-CARPET DIARIES

I don't think red carpets were a thing when I was young. I mean, we saw the glamorous actors and actresses at the Academy Awards and other ceremonies on TV, I just don't remember watching them arrive at these events. I'm only mentioning this now, as I hope it will explain how completely unprepared and ridiculous Denis and I (mostly I) were when we took our wobbly first steps along the famously red-swathed walkways of the stars.

The first time I saw an actual red carpet was at a New York film premiere in the early nineties. Denis's fame was quite new, and I wasn't really paying attention to it, so I was startled by the blinding flashes of dozens of cameras and the press people calling out Denis's name. The next time was in Los Angeles, where we spent a winter while Denis was making one of his first movies.

That winter in LA was a very exciting time for us. It was the end of 1992; to put things in perspective, let me explain how 1991 had ended for us. I was seven months pregnant with Devin, our second child. Denis had decided to do his show called "No Cure for Cancer" at the Actors' Playhouse, an Off-Broadway theater downtown. He'd done the show at the Edinburgh Fringe Festival the previous year and it had been a huge success. When we moved back to New York, he decided he should do the show there.

Denis is an optimist. I'm not. I tend to see every glass as half-empty, every cloud with a pitch-black lining, so when he told me he would be doing less traveling to other cities doing stand-up and wouldn't that be great to have him around more while he rehearsed for the show, my response was to burst into tears and say, "NO!" I was pregnant, so I was emotional, but paying for food and shelter was more important now than ever. How would we pay the rent without his income from stand-up gigs? "What if critics come?" I asked him. "What if newspapers review it?" He told me that was the whole point of doing the show, and I realized I'd married a madman. Yes, the audiences had loved the show at the Edinburgh Festival, but this was New York.

My mother came to help for a week or so before our daughter was due. During that week, I was informed by our health insurance company that our policy was about to lapse because we were behind on our payments, and we had been served a legal "notice to vacate" our apartment because we were behind on rent. This was the era of answering machines, and I always waited until my mother was in the bathroom or asleep before I played the messages from the collection agency that had taken over our student loans and the other agency that was trying to collect on a credit card we had overrun. Oh, and the IRS. We owed them, too.

Then the show opened, and it received rave reviews. Our daughter was born, and six weeks later we were staying in a beautiful villa in Puerto Vallarta, Mexico, for a month. Denis was making his first movie. Our debts had been paid with the first check for that movie.

So, 1992 was an exciting year. That December, we moved to Los Angeles for three months because Denis was making another movie and the production had rented a beautiful house in Santa Monica for us. In addition to the house, they were providing us with a car. Denis was given some options and chose the largest one because we had two car seats. When a production assistant met us at the house and handed us the keys to the gleaming black Lincoln Town Car, we couldn't believe our eyes. Denis said he wished his father were alive to see us driving around in this luxurious car, and I nodded with tears of gratitude. It was equipped with the first navigational system I'd ever used, and whenever we reached our destination, a female voice with a very posh accent declared: "You have arrived." Yes, I thought each time. Yes, we have.

One of our first nights in LA, we were invited to have dinner with Denis's agent and a famous couple. By happenstance, we pulled up to the restaurant right behind the agent and his wife. When they got out of their sports car, they were roaring with laughter.

"That's brilliant, Leary!" the agent said. "So funny!"

The valet was chuckling too when Denis handed him the keys. "I love comedians," he said. "My wife and I are huge fans, she'll love this."

We soon realized that people are driven in Town Cars—but don't typically drive them. We had no idea that they were like limos. The agent and parking valet had thought we were being hilariously ironic, so we went with that. We spent the next three months joking about how Denis had insisted on the Town Car because—*who drives a Town Car—ha, ha, ha!* Somebody on the production crew later told Denis that they'd assumed we had a personal driver on our "staff" when we asked for the Town Car.

Denis was driven to work each day by a teamster, and I used the car to do stuff with the kids and I can't tell you how much we loved that car. Until the night we attended our first Los Angeles film premiere. We'd assumed that we would park in the garage on the same block as the movie theater. However, when we turned onto that block, we saw that the sidewalk was crowded with spectators and there was a long line of photographers crowded around the entrance. The road was logjammed with traffic, but a police officer motioned for us to move to the lane with all the other Town Cars and limos. Denis shouted a thank-you to the cop. As we inched closer to the red-carpeted theater entrance, I touched up my lipstick.

"They must have a lot of valets parking cars at this thing," Denis marveled. It really was a long line of black vehicles. Finally, we pulled up to the red carpet. A uniformed man leapt from the sidewalk and opened the back door. There he found two empty car seats, toys, scattered Cheerios, banana peels, and an enormous box of diapers. When we turned to grin at him from the front seat, I said, "It's just us," because I assumed he thought we were carpooling with another celebrity couple or something.

"Denis Leary?" the man said, now opening my door. "What happened to your driver?"

"He's dying," Denis said sincerely. We both were.

By the time that movie wrapped in early spring, I was ready to go back to New York City, and it's a good thing, because a few nights before our flight home, our Town Car was involved in a high-velocity collision with a house in Beverly Hills.

Fortunately, we weren't in the car when this happened. We were in a trendy new bar owned by Jack Nicholson. Denis and I had come with some other famous people—not as famous as Jack Nicholson, but still . . . famous enough. There was somebody from Denis's agent's office with us that night, too. Everybody was drinking a lot, except me, the recovering alcoholic who was still breastfeeding our one-year-old daughter. It got late and I was just thinking that I was ready to go home when the club's manager approached our table. He looked grim; he was looking directly at Denis. I thought my heart would stop.

"Mr. Leary?" he said, his voice quavering.

"Yeah," Denis answered. He was a little drunk, lucky him. I knew from the man's demeanor that he had devastating news.

"Oh my GOD," I cried. "What's happened? Is it the kids? Did our babysitter call?"

The manager gave me a sad smile. "No, no. Nothing like that. But there's been . . . an accident."

"What accident?" Denis demanded, scared sober.

"I'm afraid one of our parking attendants crashed your car—you were driving a . . . Lincoln Town Car, correct?"

"Yes, ha ha ha," I said, shame reclaiming its position as my core emotion. "We think it's funny to drive it around—I mean, who drives a Town Car, right?"

"Well, I'm afraid it's not drivable now. One of our attendants just drove it into a house." The manager said this quietly, but everybody at the table heard and started shouting questions.

"A HOUSE? Who hires your damn valets?"

"I'm getting my own car, give me my keys."

"What the fuck kind of valet company do you guys have? Jesus!"

"What about the driver?" I asked.

"Oh, he'll never work here again," the manager said.

"But was he injured?" I asked.

"No, he's fine, but I'm afraid your car is totaled." The manager seemed very unnerved.

Denis and I told him not to worry. It wasn't even ours; we were going to have to return it the next day. We told him they'd saved us from that hassle. We were glad to hear there was little damage to the house and especially that the driver was okay. The rental car insurance would cover everything. No problem.

The manager's relief was immense. He told us that Jack, who was there in the crowded bar someplace, knew about what happened, and he insisted that we ride home in his car.

How thrilling! Jack Nicholson was going to drop us on his way home. I thought it likely that during our ride we'd immediately become lifelong friends—Jack, Denis, and me. When we told the manager that we were staying in Santa Monica, thirty minutes away, he didn't seem concerned. He was going to go talk to Jack. Meanwhile, drinks were on the house.

A half hour passed. My boobs were going to start leaking and I was tired, so I said to Denis, "Let's find a cab."

I didn't know it, but at that time in Los Angeles, "Let's find a cab" was a real conversation stopper. Everybody in our group looked at me with frozen half smiles—they were trying to figure out if I was joking.

Denis said, "Yeah, I'll go ask that manager to call one."

The guy who worked at Denis's agency grabbed his sleeve. "Wait, no. You can't do that, man. People know who you are. There's paparazzi outside."

I, in all my innocence, said, "So?"

"You can't be seen getting into"—the agent lowered his voice to a whisper—"a fucking cab. It's not right. They wrecked your car. They owe you a ride home with a car and driver, at least."

"We weren't planning to drive the taxi," I laughed.

When nobody else laughed, I said, tugging on Denis's sleeve, "I'm sure they'll offer to pay for the cab."

"It's not about that," the agent said to Denis. "Nobody takes fucking taxis. You can't get your picture taken getting into a taxi outside this place. You're Denis fucking Leary. They wrecked your fucking car. They need to send you home with a car and driver. There's plenty lined up outside."

"Yeah, WHAT THE FUCK?" Denis said. Now he was feeling

his drinks again and was outraged. "I thought Jack Nicholson was giving us a ride. We came here with a fucking car. Jack Nicholson's guy wrecked it. Where's our fucking ride?"

It had happened. We'd stayed in LA too long, and now I was married to a diva.

The manager eventually returned. He regretted to inform us that Mr. Nicholson had left with his car and driver without telling anybody. But he'd called Jack's house and they planned to send his car and driver back for us once Jack was home.

This soothed everybody but me. I wanted to go home right then. I followed the manager away from the table and quietly asked him if he could please just call us a cab. He couldn't have been more relieved. It was obvious that Jack Nicholson had no intention of sending his car and driver back for us, and I was the only one sober enough to see that the manager had been bullshitting—trying to buy time until somebody else offered us a ride. He said he'd gladly call us a cab. I returned to the table and announced that everything was all set; the car and driver were on their way.

"That's more like it," said the agent.

When the manager returned to our table he said, very grandly, "Mr. and Mrs. Leary, are you ready? Your car has arrived." It felt like we were in the movie *Sunset Boulevard*, the way he pretended that a chariot awaited us.

We said goodbye to the others at the table. They thought we were being ushered out to Jack Nicholson's car and told us to tell him they said hello. We walked into a few flashes from photographers who were loitering outside, and then we slunk into the back seat of our cab of shame. Two days later we would be heading home to New York, where riding cabs was a luxurious alternative to the subway. I couldn't wait.

We never moved to LA, but we spent a lot of time there due to Denis's work. He cowrote, produced, and starred in the FX series *Rescue Me*, which was nominated for Emmys several years in a row. He was also nominated for Golden Globes and other awards over the years, so we became somewhat adept at red carpets at these and other galas.

On the way to any awards show in LA, the traffic is bumper-to-bumper. You leave your hotel hours in advance; it takes forever to get there. You know you're close when you see the groups of protesters lining the road. They're not protesting global warming or racial injustice. They're not advocating for Black Lives Matter or #metoo. They want to protest the existence of your stinking rotten souls. Their signs warn all award nominees of their coming damnation. I once tried to photograph a sign that said we would burn in hell because we are "fornicators, masturbators, rapists, and murderers," but Denis wouldn't let me roll down the window to take the photo, because traffic was at a standstill, and he didn't want the sign holder to come over and start yelling at us about all our disgusting sins.

The traffic remains at a standstill for a long time on the way to these shows. You sit in your car and say, "Hey, there's John Hamm in the next car." "Hey, there's Viola Davis!" You worry about your lipstick and gobble mints and argue about what music should be playing on the radio and pretend that you're not a nervous wreck.

In addition to learning that celebrities don't drive their own Town Cars or limos, we also learned the hard way that it's best for the famous person or people to step out of a vehicle first. I used to open my door before Denis had a chance to open his. At the sight of my high-heeled, strappy sandals and spray-tanned calf, the fans behind their barricades cheered and photographers swarmed, crying out, "Angelina!" "NO! It's Gwyneth!" "Mariska! No, no it's Meryl! Over here, how about a smile!" When I swung the rest of me out, I waved loftily back at the crowd. No orchestra conductor has executed so dramatic a finish; the crowd's silence was swift and powerful. The photographers dropped their cameras and shot accusatory looks at me for duping them. I mumbled lame apologies for being me. Then Denis stepped out, the crowd cheered, and the photographers raised their cameras again.

Eventually, some of the regular photographers in New York and I got to know each other on a first-name basis. They would take a couple of photos of me and Denis, just to be polite, but then a producer or publicist would ask Denis to stand next to somebody famous and I'd be hustled over to the other side of the velvet rope—the side with the photographers, because I'm what's known as a "waste of editorial space." The truth is, standing with the press line is my favorite place to be at most celebrity events. There, nestled in among the reporters, cameramen, and sound guys, I've heard some of the juiciest gossip and hilarious jokes imaginable. I usually know one or two of the famous people on the red carpet and, at the urging of my new best friend/photographer, I sometimes call the famous person over to say hi. The photographer gets his close-up, then continues his jaw-dropping story about the Real Housewife who says she's fifty but is sixty and is about to be arrested for trafficking fake Hermès handbags to her rich friends in some kind of Ponzi scheme.

"Hey, the toxicology test just came back on you-know-who," another photographer will say. "KATIE! KATIE, look over here!"

"No, who?" I beg. Then I notice they're calling to an actress I know. I wave her over to us. We hug, tell each other it's been ages; she poses for the photographers, and when she leaves, I'm paid for my efforts with an earful about you-know-who, who snorted too much you-know-what even though he just got out of you-know-where.

One year, I was standing with the reporters in the press line at a pre-Emmy party. Denis was making his way down the line of photographers toward us when a young TV interviewer told me she thought it would be fun if I interviewed Denis instead of her. That did sound like fun. I took the microphone, and just then Cloris Leachman was about to walk past.

I had never met Cloris Leachman, but she was on a very short list of people I'd love to meet before I, or they, died. I called out, "Ms. Leachman!"

The TV interviewer was young; she had no idea who Cloris Leachman was. Cloris had no idea that I didn't work for the entertainment network whose logo was on my microphone, and I ended up interviewing her instead of Denis because I get to talk to Denis all the time and I had a million questions for Cloris. I started by asking her about how she got started acting, then her parts on the stage, *The Last Picture Show*, *Mary Tyler Moore*, and I had just begun a probing question about *Young Frankenstein*, when the real TV interviewer snatched her mic back and angrily waved Cloris away.

"This isn't the fucking Actor's Studio," she snapped at me. "No one cares about Betty White's life story, *Jesus*."

At major awards shows, I stay with Denis, not the photographers. I'm forced to cling to him during the long succession of interviews, because people are crowding us from all sides and I'm afraid if I let go, he'll be swept away by the human tide, and I'll have to force my way back upstream to our empty car.

There are bleachers filled with photographers on both sides of the red carpet at awards shows, and the red carpet is not a straight line to the theater, as I had once thought. It's more like a corn maze, with zigs and zags, crazy wrong turns with abrupt dead ends in front of bleachers of screaming fans. The producers of various shows like *E!* and *Entertainment Tonight* hustle us from place to place, asking us to wait in line to step onto their little stage to be interviewed, and we meet people from our favorite shows while waiting. It's still only midafternoon, we're drenched in sweat, and my dress is soaked like everybody else's, but it's fun, I cannot lie.

When Denis was one of the nominees at an award show, I was loaned or given a gown by designers like Vera Wang and Calvin Klein, because these companies knew that Joan Rivers or Ryan Seacrest would ask me "who I was wearing," in front of millions of people. The year we were invited to our first White House Correspondent's Dinner, Calvin and Vera couldn't have cared less what I wore, so I went shopping.

I was more excited about the White House Correspondents' Dinner than any other event we'd attended. This is an annual event in honor of the media covering politics, and it involves a bit of good-natured roasting of the president and others. It was Barack Obama's first year as our president. I needed to find something to wear, so I hit a few department stores to try on some things. At Bergdorf's, I breezed in and out of the showrooms, dazzled by the beautiful finery all around me. I don't usually shop in the evening wear department.

A coolly reserved, elegant saleswoman asked me what the occasion was, and when I told her, she showed me to a spacious dressing room and proceeded to bring me gowns and dresses designed by Valentino, Oscar de la Renta, and others. Oh, there were some beautiful gowns. I tried on a very slimming black dress; it was perfect. I glanced at the price tag. At first, I thought the price was fourteen thousand dollars, so I chuckled, fished my reading glasses from my purse, and then read the price again. It was fourteen thousand dollars.

When the saleswoman returned to my dressing room, I told her that I hadn't really planned on spending that much. She tried to persuade me—hadn't I said I was going to the Correspondents' Dinner? Wasn't my husband an actor? Finally, she managed to find a few things in the four- to six-thousand-dollar range. After seeing the prices on the first batch she had brought in, these dresses seemed like absolute steals, and I can't tell you how close I came to purchasing a forty-nine-hundred-dollar gown.

"It's handmade; see all of the delicate stitching. It looks like it costs twice that!" said one of the other salespeople. A small crowd of them had gathered—things seemed slow in the overly priced evening wear department that day.

"It looks like it was made for you!" another exclaimed.

Then, the zinger that has made me purchase more outlandish rags than I care to admit: "Not many people can wear that dress. You really do it justice!"

When I heard that comment, I stepped back from the mirror. I squinted my eyes a little so as not to see the rolls of flesh bulging out in front of my armpits where the dress cut into me so tightly it left welts that remained for hours.

It really is perfect, I thought. *Who else could wear this dress?*

Then I lapsed into a short reverie about the way the dress would transform me—perhaps forever; how it would deliver me, finally, onto the international stage. The photographers would fight each other to catch a photo of me. "Mr. Leary!" they would cry out in exasperation at my husband. "Could you step aside? We'd like a shot of just Ann and the gown, please!"

I imagined having to fend off the advances of one of the sexiest men on earth, himself—President Obama.

"Nobody else could wear that gown. I'm telling you, nobody," the president would gush as we submitted to the press corps' demand that we pose for one more photograph together.

"Please, sir, remember yourself... I'm married, and so are you!"

I would whisper later, as he whirled me around the dance floor and nuzzled my ear.

I had the saleswoman put the gown on hold and left the store. When I arrived out on the street, I came to my senses. There was an old man sitting on a piece of cardboard, surrounded by his filthy belongings. He had a cup in front of him where a few people had thrown some coins.

I was about to spend five grand on a dress that I would wear once.

I wore a different black dress; one I'd worn a few times, and I donated the money I would have spent on the other dress to a hunger relief organization. I didn't meet the president, but we sat at a great table. I sat next to the actor—oh, what's his name? He was in *The Office*. Not the British version, the American one. Such a nice guy. And Nora O'Donnell was at our table. I'm pretty sure it was Nora O'Donnell.

This drives Denis insane. I don't know who anybody is.

Years ago, at a dinner party, I was seated next to a very sweet, nebbishy-looking guy who seemed a little out of his element. Meg Ryan, Jon Stewart, Nora Ephron, and many others were there. Ali Wentworth and George Stephanopoulos were also at our table. They had been dating for less than two weeks. They're friends of ours, and now their daughters are in college, but how can that be? This party seems like it was yesterday. The thing about humiliating situations is that they always feel so fresh. Memories of my finer moments such as . . . well . . . none come to mind right now, but they all seem to fade. Shameful moments have a way of crystallizing in my memory. They're preserved, perfectly intact, forever.

My shy dinner companion at that party was concerned that there wouldn't be anything for him to eat, as he was vegan. He was so quiet and unassuming. He didn't seem to know anybody, and I assumed that he was somebody's plus-one. A famous actor's cousin, maybe, visiting from out of town. I realized he was overwhelmed by the dazzling luminaries in the room, so I decided to take him under my wing. I asked one of the waitstaff to prepare him a salad, and then I explained to him who all the important people were. On his other side was a very famous actress. I told him that he shouldn't be shy—he should introduce himself to her. He told me he already had. At one point I asked him what he did for work. He told me that he was a musician.

"Wow, that's really cool," I said, imagining him in an orchestra pit, his upper lip quivering above a flute, or perhaps on a subway platform strumming on a mandolin.

When we left the party, Denis and I shared a ride with Jon Stewart and his wife, Tracey.

"What was Moby like?" Tracey asked me when we were all in the back of the car. Denis and Jon leaned in toward me with expectant smiles.

"Moby was there?" I asked. "I love Moby!"

I'd been listening to a Moby playlist all summer; it was pretty much all I listened to that summer. I guess I'd never seen his photograph, because—yes, Moby had been my sweet, shy dinner companion.

I began confessing to the others, in a voice rising hysterically, that I had just schooled Moby on the ins and outs of fame. I had just promised Moby that if he had a sample CD of one of his songs, I would personally make sure my husband, Denis, listened to it.

"Denis Leary," I'd said to him, with a humble little laugh. I don't like name-dropping.

Then I said, and my face is flaming now just typing these words: "I can't promise anything, but if he likes one of your songs—who knows, maybe he'll use it on his show." I think I even offered some wisdom about how, in show business, it's not what you know, it's who you know.

God bless Moby. He didn't laugh in my face and tell me he'd never heard of Denis Leary or his damn TV show. He thanked me for my thoughtfulness. He asked me about myself.

This reminds me of something else I've learned on the sidelines of fame. Famous people have an undeservedly bad reputation as a group. They're always accused of being entitled, stupid, selfish, and narcissistic. Many are. But the most entitled jerks at the Emmys or the Golden Globes or even celebrity-filled dinner parties tend to be actors who people besides me don't recognize, along with lawyers, agents, and certain publicists. These jerks will snatch a seat away from an elderly woman with a walker because she doesn't belong in the VIP area. They push and shove their way to the front of the press line where nobody wants to take their picture. The most talented celebrities, in my experience, tend to be the most generous and kind. I'm talking about Michael J. Fox and Tracy Pollan, now. I'm talking about Morgan Freeman, Meryl Streep, Robert De Niro—and all the other gentle giants of the celebrity kingdom. They're thoughtful and kind; they wait their turn in line. They offer their seat to the pregnant or elderly. They turn away from the famous actress at a dinner party to say to the awkward, bumbling actor's wife—the nobody seated next to them—"Tell me about yourself."

EMPTY NEST

When we dropped our oldest, Jack, at college, we were all very cheery while we unloaded the car. Then Denis, Devin, and I helped Jack carry his stuff up to his dorm room. We marveled at the closet space and groaned at the thinness of the mattress. Eventually we found ourselves looking around the room with forced smiles.

"Is that everything?" Denis and I said, over and over again. "Maybe we left something in the car. That can't be everything."

We had arrived at the moment we had dreaded, not just all summer, but for the past eighteen years. It was time to say goodbye to our son's childhood.

"What about your winter jacket? What about your soap?" I cried. "I feel like we forgot something."

But it was all there—all the stuff of this boy. His guitar, his sneakers, his sheets and towels and shaving gear, his great sense of humor, his optimism, his grace and kindness, his intuitive wisdom, his big generous heart. There it all was. There was nothing else for us to do. It was time to go.

Two years later, we had to take our daughter, Devin, to her college. Again, I was overcome with emotion when I realized the moment had arrived. I thought about her birth and the nurse who helped deliver her. The nurse had plopped her onto a table and tossed her limbs from side to side as she rubbed her tiny chest. "Just helping her breathe," the nurse said cheerfully. *Not so rough*, I thought, but said nothing. One must breathe. *Tenderly*, is what I kept thinking at that nurse, the tears running down my face. *Tenderly*.

I remembered the first time she drove away from our home with her new driver's license. Music was blaring from the car windows—intrusive thoughts of screeching brakes and shattered glass were exploding in my head. "Slowly," I called out to her. *Slowly*, I thought over and over when she was no longer in sight.

"Why do I feel like we forgot something?" I sobbed as we drove away from Devin's new home—her college dorm. "What did we forget to do?"

Denis pulled the car over. After a few minutes I composed myself and said, "I'm okay, you can keep driving." But Denis didn't say anything. He didn't start driving.

"You can go, I'm fine," I sniffed.

Then I heard a strange sound, a loud hacking and choking sound coming from his direction. I looked over and saw that the man had buried his face in his hands and was bawling like a baby.

"She just looked . . . so small," he said, and I knew what he meant. Devin is on the tall side, but she looked so tiny and vulnerable when she walked away from our car. There she went, up those cold stone steps that led into that monstrous, gothic-looking dormitory. There she went, with her backpack and cell phone, her wisdom and humor, her quick, inquisitive mind, her sweet smile. She was born an old soul, with an uncanny knowledge about people. She always loved animals and all fragile things. She could walk when she was nine months old. Now she was surrounded by strangers. Why had we taught her to walk? We drove home so slowly. We dreaded returning to our empty house, but eventually, of course, we were there.

I watched a *Seinfeld* rerun as I cooked our dinner that evening. My eyes were swollen and my nose raw from crying. When the meal was ready, Denis shuffled into the kitchen and automatically turned the TV off. "Wait," I said, and then I uttered the words my husband had waited twenty years for me to say: "Let's watch TV while we eat."

And that's when the fun began.

In our home, while the kids lived with us, television had been banned during mealtime and on school nights. We had family dinners every night. This was a time to talk to one another—to connect. That first night of our empty nest, and every night that followed, Denis and I didn't ask about each other's day or discuss current events. Instead, we laughed at the TV with mouths full of food. We slouched over our plates and rested our elbows on the table. We ate with our fingers if we felt like it—and we usually felt like it. When one of us needed the salt, we lurched across the table and grabbed it without asking for it to please be passed. We rolled our corn in the butter. We slurped the last drops of soup from our bowls. We still placed our napkins on our laps—not because it was polite, but because we made such a mess and wanted to protect our clothes.

Within days, our house became a sort of hedonist temple. We swore, not just by accident when slamming a finger in a drawer or stubbing a toe. We swore all the time. One day, I needed to get something out of the dryer, so I ventured out of our bedroom in my underwear. I did my usual red-faced dash to the dryer, and then stopped. Why was I being stealthy? The people who reacted to my body with retching sounds were gone. The one who liked me in my underwear was charging up the stairs to get a closer look. Before long, we walked around our house as naked as jaybirds. We had sex whenever we wanted, wherever we wanted. We sang loudly with music—our music. We danced, not as if nobody was watching, but because nobody was watching (and laughing). We gossiped about our friends, made fun of people's accents or the way people dressed. We were petty and closed-minded again! We hadn't been aware of how hard it was being good, until we no longer had to be good. It had been exhausting. Now we were free.

I'm sure many people don't alter their behavior much when they become parents. I think those are people who are naturally altruistic, conscientious, and polite. We're not really like that. But for twenty long years we tried hard to act as if we were. We wanted to set an example for our children—a good example. For instance, whenever I gossiped on the phone with my sister, I'd have to change the subject if my daughter walked into the room. It wasn't just because I didn't want her to hear what I was saying; I didn't want her to hear me saying it. Because gossiping isn't nice. Eventually, it became easier to just not gossip very much. Denis and I had to act like better people, and over time, it became less of an act. If we lost at tennis or Scrabble, while playing with the kids, Denis and I had to smile and congratulate the winners, instead of openly sulking and accusing each other of cheating as we had always done before we had children. Eventually, by pretending we were good sports, we became good sports. (Well, everything is relative. We tried, that's my point.)

During the two decades that we raised our kids, my husband and I were better people. We weren't perfect, of course, but we worked at being the best people we could be. Our two children deserved better than us—we knew this as soon as they were born. So, we worked hard at being better. Now I understand that this wasn't just good for our children, it was good for us. But it required a lot of work. So, we're in semiretirement. When the kids come home to visit, we put on our clothes, clean up our language, and turn off the TV during dinner. They know we swear like pirates and slouch around in our underwear when they're not here. They know that we're lazy, petty, and sloppy. But we try to rein it in when they're here. It's good for us to try to be good during these visits. Just for old times' sake. Just for the children.

OPEN HOUSE

After twenty years in our Connecticut house, Denis and I decided it was time to downsize. Our kids were grown, and the house was more than we needed, so we listed it with a local real-estate broker. While we were excited to move on to the next phase of our lives, it was bittersweet. I cried a little when I made the slideshow that I'd decided should be playing on our TV as the first prospective buyers strolled through. It was autumn when we listed it—certainly a beautiful time of year at our place—but I wanted the buyers to see how enchanting their new home would be the rest of the year. Here was the front porch in summer—the rocking chairs with the faded paint facing out over the shady lawn and the pond below. It was too bad Brian, our broker, didn't like owners to be home when he shows properties—I would have told the buyers that we didn't know the pond was there when we bought the house. The field surrounding it was overgrown with scrappy trees and rough underbrush then. Now it's surrounded by a grassy meadow and three towering willow trees. We bought the willows as saplings soon after we moved in, and planted them there ourselves. Now they were three stories tall.

The next slide showed the same view in early spring—you can see blossoms on the apple trees just beyond the pond. Daffodils dot the lawn and flower beds. Oh, and here was a lovely shot of the sloping horse pasture, verdant green in summer, and, in the next shot, silvery white on a crisp winter morning. Fresh, glistening tracks from a child's sled streak down the hillside and over the frozen pond. Next was our kitchen with a fire in the hearth. The windowpanes are framed by freshly drifted snow. We used to have fires before school, while the kids ate their breakfast. I would have liked to tell the lucky buyers about that. I imagined them watching the slides and then walking through the house as we did when we first saw it, trying to look unimpressed. I imagined her squeezing her partner's hand, as I had mine. My little squeeze said: *I will live here—or die*. His return squeeze said: *Keep it cool, remain calm so we can negotiate . . . JESUS CHRIST I LOVE THIS PLACE.*

It was supposed to be a weekend house when we bought it in 1997, but after the first summer, we couldn't bear to leave. Whenever my husband got a film job or a television deal, we made an improvement of one kind or another to the original 1850s farmhouse and surrounding acreage. A new kitchen and bedroom suite one year. A sunroom. A sport court/skating rink later. Riding trails. We were warned against putting too much money into the property. You need to think about its resale value, we were told.

"Resale!" we had laughed. We wouldn't have sold it for all the money in the world. How could we ever leave it? We had twenty

Easter egg hunts there. We had twenty Christmas trees. Our kids are grown now and live in New York City, but when they visit, we love to recall their childhood memories and we have a favorite playlist. The time the coyote was trapped in the hayloft and our little terrier Pongo chased it away. The ghost, the mice, the bats, the swallows that nested on our porch each spring. The time Clancy the wolfhound knocked down the Christmas tree right after we'd placed the star on top. One of us will say, "Remember when we let the pony in the house for the cat's birthday party?" "Remember when Jack used to walk in his sleep?" "Remember when Mom found a live bat on her pajamas?" Nobody says, "Remember when Mom battled crippling depression?" "Remember when Dad stormed out after a fight?" But they happened in that house too. All the ups and downs, the thrills and terrors of domestic life happened in that bright, messy, wonderful nest.

I wrote four books in that house; my husband wrote three television shows. Our kids went to school, then to college, and then moved to the city to work. We realized after they were gone a few years that we used only three rooms in the house. It was suddenly too big, too expensive, too much. We wanted to move closer to the city.

So Brian, our broker, scheduled an open house. As I made the slideshow to be played on the TV for the potential buyers, fluffed pillows, and plucked stray weeds from flower beds, I worried that the new owners wouldn't fully appreciate the place. They might be indoor people, which would be a shame, as the woods are magical. There are trails lined by ancient stone walls, there are wild roses and mountain laurel and a clear running brook in the woods. I fretted that they might want to tear the house down, scrapping the centuries-old beams and floorboards.

After the open house, I began packing, certain that the offers were about to start pouring in. But no offers came. Brian told us not to worry; he had lots of showings lined up. After each showing, we waited for an offer.

"We're not budging from the asking price," I declared.

"No way; it's a steal," Denis agreed.

"It's a terrible market," Brian told us.

Nothing had sold in our price range in several years. We blamed the election, we blamed the economy, but, as the weeks and then months passed with fewer viewings and no offers, we began to blame the house. "No wonder nobody wants to buy this place," I'd grumble if I tripped over a loose flagstone on the patio or if a few limbs fell from a tree after a storm.

"What a dump," I'd say when I opened a closet and its overstuffed contents spilled out onto the floor. My sister told me to declutter. We needed to make it neater for showings. All winter I made my way through our closets, muttering stuff like, "When in doubt, throw it out."

My mother used to declare: "Well, that doesn't owe me anything," about a nice thing that had passed its prime—a worn Burberry trench coat or an old Coach bag. If she'd used them frequently, they'd earned their keep and didn't "owe" her anything. I kept that in mind as I tossed the hopelessly frayed leather jacket that I'd worn to every event for the past ten years and the boots that had cost a fortune but had carried me through eight winters. They owed me nada. The Prada pumps that had never broken in and the Rag and Bone jeans that never fit were shiftless hangers-on, by comparison. They had never come close to earning their keep, the leeches, and somebody was going to be very pleased to find them in mint condition at the Salvation Army.

Another showing! Another call from the broker. "They loved it, it's just too big. They're a retired couple. It's really a place for a young family, but most young families can't afford it."

We lowered the price.

All his life, my husband had wanted a skating rink. I'd wanted a horse for as long as I could remember. We bought a horse, then another and another. We built a barn and a skating rink. We rode and skated with our kids and our friends. We had skating parties. We had hockey tournaments. Even after my decluttering, I'd open a closet and see an empty oxygen tank from the years when I volunteered as an EMT, a brace from when a horse broke my knee, part of our son's old drum set, a tiny dance costume.

We lowered the price again.

Finally, an offer came. It was lower than what we were asking. Much, much lower than what we'd originally asked. We didn't feel like we could accept it. We'd grown up in a time when parents bought a house for thirty thousand dollars, and not many years later, sold it for twice that. We had this idea that real estate always appreciates. This house owed us—if not what we'd originally hoped, at least what we'd put into it. If we accepted the offer, we'd be taking a loss on the place. Yes, we needed money like everybody else, but what troubled me more than the prospect of losing some of the money that we'd put into the house was this embarrassment I felt at the sense that we'd squandered it. We were fools to have built a hockey rink! It was not an asset to the property—there were ugly maintenance sheds next to it—any prospective buyer must have calculated the costs of removing those eyesores. The barn, fencing, riding ring—these had been expensive to build, but not a lot of people have horses. So, when Brian urged us to consider the offer, I had to confront the dreadful shame that had been building slowly during that entire year when nobody wanted to buy our house.

For the past several months, whenever I left so that Brian could show it, I imagined a couple walking through and shaking their heads in dismay. I imagined the woman squeezing her partner's hand. Her little squeeze said: *Gross.* And his returning squeeze said: *I know, imagine wasting all your money on this dump instead of buying Apple stock.* Brian told us that the couple who'd made the offer had seen the property several times and loved it. They were a young family. This was at the very top of their price range and they wouldn't go any higher. They had a little girl who loved horses. Apparently, she burst into tears every time they had to leave after seeing it. We told him we'd get back to him.

"That whole little girl crap is just a play on our emotions," Denis said.

"Yeah," I replied, and then went up to the barn to tuck in the horses for the night.

It was late autumn again. When we'd first moved there, I used to walk up the hill to the barn with a flashlight. Then, when there was a full moon, I didn't need a flashlight. Eventually I could walk up there without a flashlight, moon or no moon. I could walk there in the dark because every step had been programmed into my brain. I had spent two decades walking up to check the horses every night before going to bed. I'd top up their water buckets and toss them a flake of hay. I'd look out at the moonlit field and wonder how it came to be that we were able to live in such a perfect, beautiful place.

So that night I walked up to the horse barn in the pitch-dark, my two dogs padding along at my side. I groaned as I pulled the sliding door open—the track was rusted and bent, and it hadn't opened properly in years. I threw hay to my horse and pony and listened to their peaceful munching. I liked to stand there and listen to them in the night, so I leaned on the old, weathered barn door and looked out at the fields. We needed to replace some of the fencing if the house didn't sell by spring. A tree had fallen in a recent storm—a big tree. That mess had to be cleaned up.

The little girl loves it here, I thought. *She cried when she had to leave.* We'd spent twenty years there. Nobody lives anywhere for free. Yes, we'd spent more than others thought it was worth, but it was worth it to us at the time. And it hit me just then; I don't know why it hadn't occurred to me before: this house didn't owe us anything.

Before the closing, Brian told us that the buyers were planning to surprise their little girl that afternoon. They were going to pretend that they were just going to the house for another look, but when they went upstairs, all her things would be in her new bedroom.

Maybe it was a fiction, but I love fiction. We left that day and never looked back.

THE GREENHOUSE EFFECT

We purchased our current home from the estate of Linda Rodgers Emory, who'd recently passed away. Linda Emory was the daughter of Richard Rodgers—*the* Richard Rodgers of Rodgers and Hart/Rodgers and Hammerstein musical fame. This Richard Rodgers connection was something the real-estate brokers mentioned more than once when we were shown the house. The score from *The Sound of Music* played from a portable speaker as we wandered through, but I wasn't paying attention. I'd fallen in love the moment we pulled into the driveway and was trying to mute my thunderous *live here or die* intrusive thoughts so that we would be in a better negotiating position. It's not a particularly small or large house, but I've never lived in a place I love more.

I don't think much about the spiritual world, but I believe Mrs. Emory might be in this house with us in a supernatural sense. She's definitely here in the natural sense. From what I've learned, Mrs. Emory (yes, I call her Mrs. Emory, not Ms. Emory or Linda) was musical, like her father, and she was also a passionate gardener.

We bought the house in February, when the gardens were dormant and covered in snow. There's a little lean-to greenhouse attached to the older part of the house, where she had left behind dozens of terra-cotta pots. I've never had much success with houseplants. I've always been better with children and dogs because I understand their needs. In the past, I would buy a plant—I laugh now, because until we moved here, all green leafy things in pots were plants to me, I had no idea what any were called. I poured water on them and put them in places I thought would look pretty. I watered them when I thought of it, and when they expired, I assumed that their time had come—that plants didn't have long life expectancies. Mine seemed to grow old and die within three to six months.

I decided Mrs. Emory's little greenhouse was going to be my office. It's bright and quiet—the perfect place for me to write. I bought a houseplant for my desk because it was technically a greenhouse, and I continued working on a novel I'd been researching and writing for several years. That spring, Mrs. Emory's perennials rose from the beds around the house and burst into bloom. We had no idea what she had planted, so it was like a thrilling performance that went on and on, all summer and into the fall. She'd choreographed the gardens so that something was always flowering. The daffodils and snowdrops were the prelude, then the shimmying irises and peonies appeared, as if on cue. Exit peonies, enter daylilies. Ta-da!

There were a few stoneware planters on the patio that were filled with dirt that first winter. I thought Mrs. Emory's family hadn't noticed them or forgot to put them away the previous fall. They were heavy because they were packed with all that old dirt. One spring day, I noticed little green stems sprouting from the dirt. Then they bloomed! The pots had been planted with gorgeous perennials that still bloom every year on our patio. *What an unexpected and thoughtful gift* is what I would have written to Mrs. Emory if she were still alive. Instead, I say it to my beloved potted flowers that arrive on the exact same week in May every year.

When you move into a new old house, even though it's empty, there are traces of its former residents. In this house, there were mysteries. There's a safe in our basement. I emailed Mrs. Emory's son to ask him about it. He was sure it had been emptied and gave me what he thought might be the combination so we could use it, but the combination didn't work. I planned to get a locksmith to open it, but never did. I like to think there's something Mrs. Emory dearly treasured inside—not money or jewels, but perhaps a poem or a song—something that will seem like a key to her very soul, a message from the hereafter. I'm afraid to open it because what if there's nothing?

Another mystery was a shower in the hallway next to the greenhouse. The other showers and bathrooms in this house were a little dated, but this shower is so on-trend, it could be photographed for an interior design magazine with its white subway tiles and gleaming showerhead and faucets. The only issue we've ever had with it is that nobody, except our smallest dog, fits inside. It's about two feet in diameter and sits above a small cabinet rather than on the floor. It's about four feet high and has a removable plexiglass panel in front that allows you to fill it with water to make a small bath. But for whom? I discovered a sliding pocket door hidden in a doorframe that separates this room from the greenhouse, and at the bottom of that door is a swinging pet door, too small for most dogs. It was a cat door, I realized. The shower must have been made for cats. I'm not a cat person, but I decided that Mrs. Emory must have kept fancy show cats she washed and groomed in that shower, and that's what I told all our puzzled guests.

As it turns out, I was wrong. Something happened after we'd lived in the house for about a year that not only solved the mystery of the shower—it changed my life. I had a plant that I now know was a golden pothos, but was then just the plant in the greenhouse. I noticed white lint-like matter on a few leaves, and when my mother was visiting, she told me they might be a type of pest. I took a photo of the plant and drove to our local nursery. When I showed the photo to a woman working there, she said, "You have mealybugs." Then she looked me in the eye and said in a hushed but sympathetic tone, "It's nothing to be ashamed of, dear, they're common and easy to get rid of."

It hadn't occurred to me that I should feel shame until she made it seem as if my plant had contracted an STD. She sold me a bottle of spray to eradicate the nasty bugs, and it was on our way to the cash register that I found my gateway plant—the first in what I proudly call my houseplant collection, but my family considers more of a hoarding/addiction situation. I saw a plant with beautiful purple-and-green variegated foliage and asked what it was. This woman, who had thought I might be ashamed of tiny bugs on a plant, told me the Latin name of the plant and then said, quite unashamedly, something that sounded like, "It's a wandering Jew." I was sure I'd misunderstood her; I have terrible hearing, so I asked if it was easy to care for. This opened the door to something akin to a pet adoption interview. Where did I plan to put it? Would it be in a sunny area, or a less sunny area? It liked water, but not too much water. It liked sun, but it needed to be introduced gradually. She thought we were a good match because it was a fast grower and an easy keeper.

I brought my *Tradescantia zebrina* home and put it in a sunny spot. I was careful that it got enough sun, but not too much. It grew so fast that I soon had to transplant it into one of Mrs. Emory's larger planters. When I went to the nursery to buy potting soil, a plant with brightly colored leaves caught my eye. I read the little placard poking out of its pot. It was a Calathea medallion. It didn't like too much sun. It liked humidity. It liked moist soil but hated to be too wet.

It liked things and hated things. So do I! I was in love.

The nursery owner remembered me and tried to warn me off. "It's not really a beginner plant," she said. "Why not a nice philodendron?" But I bought the sensitive Calathea that liked things just so. I would not keep it on my desk, I would keep it on a shadier shelf. I would mist its pretty leaves. I have it still, and several other Calatheas, too. I also have philodendrons, monsteras, ferns, snake plants, Alocasias. I have quite a few varieties of pothos because they're so easy to propagate.

I began propagating plants during the first winter of Covid, when many shops were closed. I placed a few cuttings in a glass of water and watched them do nothing, day after day, while cable news programs blasted the tragically mounting Covid deaths. Then a miracle—tiny white nubbins poked out of the cuttings. Once the roots emerged, they grew, it seemed by the hour. They appeared to be reaching out to me when their tips touched the inside of the glass that I held and turned in my hands. Oh, and the shower? It's for plants! It's the perfect size for even my larger plants. Showering leaves regularly is the way to keep mealybugs and spider mites away—that's why Mrs. Emory gave them the prettiest shower in the house.

I read about horticulture as I grew and potted my plants. I learned that many houseplants are cultivars, meaning that they've been bred for specific traits. I was still writing my novel *The Foundling*, which is about the eugenics era, when "inferior" or "unfit" people were considered as dangerous and invasive as poison ivy. They were locked in asylums or sterilized so they couldn't reproduce. My grandmother worked in such a place. She's no longer alive, but I felt her and Mrs. Emory with me when I hit snags in the plot. I sensed Mrs. Emory especially when I worked late at night, surrounded by a silent, understanding audience that photosynthesized and cleansed the air for me as I worked.

I had googled Mrs. Emory when we first moved here and was pleased to learn that her father had written the song "My Funny Valentine," which our friend Julie sang for my husband and me at our wedding. But now I wanted to know about Linda Rodgers Emory, not her father. I read a few interesting profiles written about her and her obituary. I discovered that Mrs. Emory was loving and giving, she was philanthropic and creative, but she also struggled, as I have, with shyness and bouts of severe depression. Some quick math revealed that she moved here when she was about my age. The trees, the flowers, the gardens, and the greenhouse that lift my spirits each day—had creating them lifted hers?

I'm not into musicals and show tunes, but I heard the Rodgers and Hammerstein song "Edelweiss" around Christmastime last year. I was in my happy place—the local plant shop—just browsing. The tune stuck with me; it's one of those songs that takes root. Later, I was still singing it as I tried to rearrange some plants on my greenhouse "desk" to make room for my laptop. Like I said, I'm not really into spirituality or show tunes, but I got a little teary as I hum-sang to all my green darlings, my tender foundlings, and to the spirit of Mrs. Emory too: "*Blossom of snow, may you bloom and grow, bloom and grow forever.*"

TRAVEL TRAVAILS

We traveled much more as a family when we were a younger family, often to locations where Denis was working. When the kids were infants and toddlers, we took them with us everywhere, and the only part that we found difficult was that the car seats and extra gear required that we check our luggage. We hate checking our luggage.

By the time the kids were old enough to walk through airports, we carried our stuff and they tried to carry theirs. The last time I was in a luggage area was in the late 1990s. I'm not sure why, but Denis and I feel that checking luggage when flying is an indication of some kind of deep moral failing. We take a perverse pride in the idea that we could probably tour all seven continents with the regulation two light carry-ons.

My proudest achievement in this regard was a trip we took during the kids' spring break when they were in kindergarten and second grade. Denis was shooting a movie in Puerto Rico. We were going to meet him in Puerto Rico, then go to Amsterdam with him, where he would begin work on another film. His schedule for the Amsterdam shoot included a week off during which we would visit Venice. Then the kids and I would return to New York, and Denis would return to Amsterdam. This was late February, and I successfully packed carry-on bags for three people and two different climates. We had swimsuits and parkas, nice clothes and casual, and we never checked a thing. To be honest, two of the people wore very small clothing and we had a stroller that didn't count as luggage in those days, so it was easy to schlep our bags through airports.

It took me a while to figure out how to pack so lightly for a trip. I used to pack too much. When planning a trip, I'd open my closet and see a dress that I'd splurged on but had only worn once, and some very chic heels that for some reason, I'd also not had the opportunity to show off. I'd pack these and other things, many other things, but rarely the few things I tended to wear every day. I wanted to wear my nicest things while traveling. I'd pack several sweaters, jackets, and multiple pairs of jeans if we were going to a cold place like Ireland or England. Huge sun hats, cover-ups, dresses, jeans, tennis rackets, sneakers, and many shoe options if we were visiting a tropical place.

Inevitably, when we arrived at our destination, I would put on that designer dress and realize why I never wore it. It made my stomach look fat and my ass look skinny. Which they were, but why accent those things? Those fancy heels killed my feet; that's why I never wore them at home. I finally realized that at home, I tend to wear the same things, cycling through about three different variations of my most flattering tops with my favorite jeans. When we go out, I have a dress and a few skirts that always feel right. Now, those are the things I pack. Here are a few more quick tips to traveling light:

- Wear your biggest shoes on the plane. If it's winter, wear the one pair of great boots that you wear all the time, hopefully a pair that can be worn with a dress or jeans and don't have heels that are too high for running through airport terminals. Then tuck your favorite flats and one dressy pair of shoes in with your clothes. If it's summer and you are a runner or tennis player, wear those sneakers on the plane and pack one flat and one dressy shoe option in your carry-on.

- The carry-on should have wheels if you are female. My husband won't do a wheeled carry-on, I have no idea why. He also won't wear anything resembling a sandal. He's worn work boots to the beach. I wish I was joking.

- Roll up all clothing. Do not fold. This is a major space-saver and keeps clothes from wrinkling.

- Pack one pair of jeans, one dressier pant option (if you must), several tops, a skirt, a dress, and tons of underwear. Maybe socks and tights if it's going to be cold. I love scarves and pack my favorite. That way, I can dress up the T-shirts and other plain stuff I wear.

- While traveling through airports, wear as much as you can. If you must bring a bulky sweater or jacket, wear them. Airplanes are freezing. Again, your clunkiest shoes are worn, the smaller shoes are packed.

- Most important, pack what you wear all the time. Leave your fantasy wardrobe in the closet. There's a reason you never wear those things.

Or check your luggage. You'll probably still get to go to heaven.

When we visited European cities with our kids, we usually hired a guide for a few hours or a day, to make it educational for all of us. On a trip to Paris in 2004, we took a trip to the Château de Versailles with an amiable guide named Didier. When we arrived, Didier parked the car, we followed him inside and purchased our tickets. Then, Didier led us up some beautiful marble steps into a vast hall covered with murals, and I cried.

I must interrupt my story here to explain something. When my kids were little, I read a lot about child development, and I learned that children go through certain stages after which they are somewhat able to regulate their emotions. I completely skipped these stages. They're supposed to happen around five or six, but I think I spent the whole time playing with kittens and watching the *Land of the Giants* or something, and the stages passed me right by. As a result, I struggle, on occasion, with the whole emotional-regulation thing. I tell this now, because when we entered this first vast, muraled hall at the Palace of Versailles and I started crying, I don't mean that my eyes misted up, or that I had to wipe away a tear. No, I burst into wracking sobs. I tried to wipe the tears away, but they were streaming down my face. Devin noticed them and grabbed Jack, saying, "Don't look at Mom, it's too embarrassing. DO NOT look at Mom." They ran ahead. Denis caught a glimpse of me and stopped walking so he could study the ceiling mural very carefully.

Since my family had scattered, Didier had only me to begin his tour with. We walked side by side, and it took a few minutes for him to discover why his friendly questions were met with my silence. When he saw that I was sobbing too hard to speak, he asked if I'd just received bad news about a death in the family or something. I sputtered, tears spraying everywhere: "No, no. I wasn't ready for it, that's all. It's so . . . beautiful."

It's not really my favorite interior design style, Versailles. I like more of a boho vibe, personally, but my senses were overwhelmed by the enormity and brilliance of everything—the tapestries and murals, the musculature of the painted horses, warriors, gods and goddesses, the sparkling chandeliers, the leaded windows leading out to the gardens. I just needed a minute. When I'd recovered, my family joined us again and we listened to Didier describe the lifestyles of Kings Louis the XIV, XV, and XVI.

My favorite thing (and really what little I have ever known) about French court life was all the fooling around that was going on. All the lovers and mistresses. All the illegitimate heirs. So when Didier pointed out Louis XIV's bedchamber and mentioned that a small door led to a back chamber, I chirped, "That's where he'd meet his mistress, right?"

"Well, perhaps. But there were many chambers back there . . ."

"Would his mistresses sometimes sneak into his room?" I asked breathlessly.

"No, not even his wife would visit him in his room. He would go to her."

"Interesting!" I'd say, my head spinning with all the romantic possibilities, the kids walking, fast, into the next chamber.

I did the same thing when we were shown the brothels in Pompeii and the Roman baths. Teenagers were able to listen to guides who explained about the sex menus on the walls of the Pompeii brothels, while I snickered into my hand, my cheeks flaming. It's another stage that passed me by. Maturity in general.

Visits to Italian cities are often one long crying jag for me. I'm not sad. Just overwhelmed by the rare interchange of light and shadow along the winding cobbled alleyways, the aromas wafting from cafés, the music of cathedral bells and the cathedrals themselves.

On our first morning in Florence, Denis and I decided to climb the bell tower in Il Duomo, the city's famous cathedral. All the way up, we were chatting and joking and stopping to take photos. At the top, we found ourselves in an open-aired belfry, gazing down at the unadulterated beauty of the ancient city and the purple-hued hills beyond. The sun streamed in on us in soft golden columns, and I burst into tears. Denis removed himself to the other side of the tower and returned to my side when I composed myself.

When I enter a medieval place of worship, I'm filled with awe. I find it incredible that when resources were so hard to come by, when lives were so short and so perilous, when, instead of cranes and forklifts, they had only the muscle and sweat of man and beast, cathedrals were built. These structures were glorious offerings of magnificent praise, monuments of faith and hope and love. The fact that spiritual life so clearly took precedent over the material is what makes me blink back tears and reach for my husband's hand—a hand that, in cathedrals, is usually clenched in rage.

Denis is infuriated by cathedrals. He sees in the rich ornamentation, the statuary, stained glass, and all the cold, expensive marble only the filthy corruption of the papacy and the ruthless exploitation of peasants. His view is the opposite of mine—he sees, in cathedrals, the material completely obliterating the spiritual. The nuns, visiting from points across the globe, give him chills. The smell of incense launches him into a sort of Catholic school PTSD trance, and by the second day on any trip, he just waits outside whenever I want to wander into a church.

Denis and I don't travel as much now as we did when our kids were young. When we do take a trip, we usually return to Italy, but we like to float other options first.

"Why not Istanbul?" I'll suggest.

"We never did do that African safari," Denis says, and we carry on with this charade for a few days, tossing out increasingly implausible ideas as if we're the kind of tourists who get their kicks trekking through Colombian cocaine plantations or paddleboarding in shark-infested waters. We're not adventurous, we're afraid of pretty much everything, but mostly we're afraid to visit places that we might not love. We already know that we love Italy, so if we have time to take a trip, we go there. I only cry on the first day or two. We're not Italian, but we understand the language, and because of our love of ravioli and the works of Scorsese and Coppola, we feel a sort of complicity with the Italian people. We're practically Italian, as far as we're concerned, so, especially in recent years, our European holidays have been to Italy—Venice, Rome, Florence, Tuscany, the Amalfi Coast, and most recently, Sicily.

When I said that we understand the Italian language, I didn't mean to imply that we understand all the words. No, what I mean is that we understand that we're hearing the Italian language when it's spoken. Not all the time, but most of the time, especially when we're in Italy. I do know a few words and am constantly trilling "buongiorno," "grazie," and "permesso" at hapless waiters and passersby, gesticulating wildly, all my accents on the wrong syllables and my spittle bouncing off the wrong consonants.

For our Sicily trip, we rented a car to drive around and see the sights, even though an Italian friend had advised us against this.

"Most Americans find the autostrada a little intimidating," she had warned. We are NOT most Americans, so we insisted on the rental car, and on our second day, we drove off to find a scenic town that a man named Enzo had told us about. We had met Enzo on a beach that morning. Enzo didn't speak English very well, but he managed to convey to us that we were just a short drive from the most scenic of all Sicilian towns. "It is the town in *The Godfather*—in the film, *The Godfather*," Enzo had proclaimed. And then we had to go see this real Sicilian town, this amazing *Godfather* town, so we jumped in the car and set off.

The road was winding and a little scary at first. I could see how some Americans would be frightened. "This isn't so bad," I said to Denis as he drove along. "I think it's sad that people are so limited by their fears, because you can't really experience a place until you drive its roads, just like we are. Really, it's only by poking along the byways and in and out of the sleepy villages off the beaten track that one may really get to know a place."

Denis told me that I was blocking his view. He was trying to pull out of the long steep driveway that we had just ascended. I had thought we were on a road, but it was just the driveway from our hotel.

"Nothing coming this way . . . NO STOP!" I said as three motorcycles whizzed past. The road we were entering was winding and narrow, and it was hard to see what was coming. "Okay, go now, NO WAIT!" I screamed. Then after a truck flew past, I shouted, "GO . . . GO . . . GO . . . GO . . . GO . . . STOP!"

"Sit back so I can see," Denis said through clenched teeth. And then he steered us onto the road, and we were off.

The thing to do, when you're traveling in unknown places, is to get lost right off the bat. That way you get it over with and you don't have to worry about it anymore. We tried to get on the autostrada heading north, but instead found ourselves ascending steep, winding roads leading to the lovely, but very congested, town of

Taormina. We could see how others might think driving in Sicily is scary. But we weren't afraid. We said this quite a few times as we sped around tight turns, the road dropping off thousands of feet beside us, a honking bus on our tail, and motorcycles flying at us from the opposite direction. Once we got on the autostrada, it would be better, we reassured each other.

And then we entered the autostrada.

Apparently, when they built the autostrada on this part of the Sicilian coast, the tunneling through mountains and cliffs became too tiresome, so they engineered a sort of Jetsons-style space highway. You just speed along at 90 mph, on a twisting, turning superhighway that is suspended thousands of feet—oh, I beg your pardon, meters—above the land or sea below. I really don't mind driving across bridges, because bridges have fences or walls to keep cars from falling off. The autostrada has a little guardrail. Do you know how easy it is to flip a car over a guardrail? Denis does. I know because I asked him. My head was buried between my knees, but I was able to shout, "DO YOU KNOW HOW EASY IT IS TO FLIP A CAR OVER A GUARDRAIL? Do you know that you JUST HAVE TO TOUCH THE RAIL WITH YOUR TIRE and you'll be—"

"Yup, thanks, got it," he said.

We eventually climbed a long, narrow road that led us to the hilltop village of Savoca. Savoca, in addition to being one of the locations for *The Godfather*, is a beautiful, medieval village with ancient stone walkways and views of the surrounding countryside and, in the distance, the Ionian Sea. We had lunch in a café and then happened upon the Church of San Nicolo—the church where Michael Corleone and Appolonia were married! The village of Savoca was relatively free of tourists when we first arrived, but a tour bus had just pulled up in front of the church, and we decided to have a quick look inside before the others crowded in. As we started for the main entrance, an older man approached me with a shawl and a smile. He had other, similar shawls draped across his arm. I thought he was selling them, and I admired them politely but told him that I really wasn't in the market for a shawl. He didn't speak much English but was adamant, and I admit, I got a little huffy. I wasn't going to be hoodwinked into buying a scarf, I was there to see the *Godfather* church, if he didn't mind! He did mind, very much. He wasn't selling the scarves. He pointed angrily at a placard that said, both in Italian and in English, that the Church of San Nicolo is, and has long been, a house of God, not just the *Godfather* church, and that those entering are asked to show respect by not having exposed shoulders or wearing shorts. I was wearing a sleeveless top. I apologized profusely, donned a sweatshirt, and we followed the crowd inside.

The next day, we had a young guide named Luca take us to visit Mount Etna, because we wanted to learn about the history of the volcano, and also because he would do all the driving. We'd been told it was a lovely hike up to the summit. On the way there, Luca told us about previous eruptions of Mount Etna, some of which happened during the past half century. The most devastating recent eruption was in 1992, when lava flowed down the mountain, threatening various towns and destroying numerous buildings. You can see Mount Etna for miles. Mount Etna smokes—it's a heavy smoker, but we hadn't understood, until Luca informed us, that the volcano is still active and could potentially erupt again at any moment. Maybe we were going to the wrong volcano, we told Luca. We thought you could hike up Mount Etna; we didn't know it could erupt on us.

Luca laughed at this. "Could erupt! It's a volcano and has been for millions of years. How many times does it erupt? You don't think about that. We could have earthquake—we're on earth, but you're not afraid to walk on the earth, no?"

Denis and I realized that we were in a car with a madman.

Luca took us to the village of Zafferana, which isn't too far from the base of Mount Etna. He wanted us to see a place where a miracle happened, not once, but twice. According to legend, one of the more serious Mount Etna eruptions occurred in the seventeenth century. Apparently, the villagers of Zafferana, upon seeing the lava flowing toward their homes, prayed to the Virgin Mary, and in fact carried a statue of the Blessed Mother to a point in the lava's path, just above the town. It was at that very spot that the lava stopped. So, when the 1992 eruption occurred, Luca explained, the people in the town again carried a statue of the saint to the spot where they hoped the lava would stop, and again, the lava miraculously stopped flowing at that very spot.

Luca parked the car next to a cottage at the bottom of a steep hill, and we climbed out so that we could see the place where the lava stopped. He showed us a wide ridge of hard volcanic rock—a former molten lava tsunami—that snakes down a long slope and ends just above the town, actually right behind the cottage next to where we stood. There's a small monument of the Virgin Mary there, and the people in the village keep fresh flowers placed around her feet at all times. A young woman and her two small children left the little cottage, and Luca and she greeted one another. Denis and I were marveling at how close to the house the lava had come, and Luca seemed to mistake our horror with fascination.

"Today, you'll just have time to climb up Etna, but another day, you must book a cave tour," he said. "You wear a harness and are lowered into tiny cracks in the side of the volcano, very popular," he said. He also mentioned something about Jeep tours on live lava trails, but he'd lost me at the lowering of people into the live volcano part. Had these Jeep- and cave-touring people even heard of Pompeii? I imagined a tour guide, centuries from now—perhaps a descendent of our own Luca—guiding a group of tourists through the archaeological site where we now stood. I imagined him showing the group a recently unearthed finding—the remains of a couple, so perfectly preserved you could read their American passports. I imagined the looks of disgust as he explained that nearby were the remains of two young children—crushed, along with their mother, by the American tourists who'd trampled them in their attempt to flee the flowing lava.

Our next stop was the parking lot at the base of Mount Etna. Luca was going to wait in the car while we climbed. It was now midday and very hot. Otherwise, we would have hiked all the way to the top of Mount Etna—to the part where all the smoke comes out, where all the lava will come out the next time the volcano erupts. This time we decided to just hike a little way up, past some quiet craters. Former smokers.

The landscape on Mount Etna in July is eerie and lunar, mostly barren, but with surprising waves of color from wildflowers that grow here and there in the black volcanic soil along the steep path. When we reached the summit of one of the lower craters, we stopped to take some photos. We thought we were the only people on this particular summit, but then we noticed that there were a couple of hippies sitting against their backpacks, smoking a joint. I've climbed a few small mountains and hills, and in my experience, there are always hippies smoking a joint at the summit. This friendly pair didn't speak English, but they offered to take our picture, and we took theirs.

Denis wanted to get a photo of me. "Back up," he kept saying. I backed up.

"Just a little more. A little more."

The hippies laughed and laughed. Later, when I looked at the photos, I got the joke. He had backed me up to within inches of the edge of the plateau surrounding the crater. Behind me was nothing but the faint outlines of distant craters. Another step back and I would have plummeted thousands of feet to my death, but of course Denis and the hippies stopped me. We put the camera away and just gazed down at the world below. The air around us was a thin blue color—almost white. We weren't sure if we were in a low-hanging cloud or volcanic smoke or what—probably both. It was quiet, and the air smelled faintly of sulfur, marijuana, and something else, some fragrant desert plant like eucalyptus or mimosa, and it was quite something; it was like being in heaven, and we wondered why on earth we'd been so afraid.

SHALL WE DANCE?

The studio is in a little strip mall near our town. I first noticed it on the way to the adjacent dry cleaner. I thought I heard faint music playing, and when I stopped, I saw a couple dancing on the other side of the enormous glass windows. A man in a sweater and tight jeans stood off to the side and nodded his head in time to the beat. It was the middle of the day. This wasn't Zumba or aerobics or any other kind of fitness dancing. The pair of dancers in the studio were dancing *as a pair*. They appeared to be doing a jitterbug or Charleston. I looked up at the sign and saw that this was a ballroom dancing school. I wondered why I'd never noticed the place before, sandwiched there, between a dry cleaner and nail salon that I had visited many times.

I've always wanted to be able to properly dance at a big celebration like a wedding or bar mitzvah. I mean, I can dance. I've spent my life dancing at parties and clubs, sometimes even with another person. But that was what my mother refers to as "freestyle" dancing. The closest my friends and I ever came to ballroom dancing was what we called "slow dancing" in early high school. Slow dancing usually happened at parties in somebody's parents' basement. A girl would turn off Led Zeppelin or Aerosmith and put on a James Taylor record, and another girl would lower the lights. Then, the boys, who'd been chugging beer and shoving one another in one corner, would, one by one, amble over to us girls. We were chugging something called Cold Duck and laughing like hyenas at nothing and everything in another corner. Eventually, one of the boys would grunt at me, I'd giggle-snort Cold Duck out of my nose, and then we were in a full-body hug, shuffling in little circles until the boy either scurried suddenly away or began humping my leg—both apparent reactions to a physical phenomenon that I guessed at but wasn't entirely sure.

As an adult, I've always dreaded the inevitable moment at a wedding when somebody's father or uncle asks me to dance. This is usually a wonderfully dapper fellow who thinks he'll fox-trot me around in front of his friends to show that he's still got it. After a few minutes of trying to maneuver my skip-walking form around the room, he mumbles his apologies and hustles me back to the wrong table.

When Denis and I married, we danced our obligatory first dance at our wedding. It was sort of okay, I guess. My right hand was in his hand, his other hand was on my back. Where my second hand was is anybody's guess. I had thought we would dance for a few seconds and then others would crowd onto the dance floor. Instead, we were doing an endless slow dance recital in front of everybody we knew. We smiled so hard, for so long, I thought I'd dislocated my jaw.

I understand that now, some couples take dance lessons before their weddings. If only that was a thing when we got married. Maybe it was. Getting married in a church was a thing too, but we got married in my mom's backyard because I was too socially anxious to walk down a church aisle with everybody staring at me.

Most of our friends' first dances at their weddings were like ours: a freshly betrothed couple shuffling around in a stiff dance-like pose until finally the older people—the parents and grandparents—got up on the floor and effortlessly swung and twirled each other around like nobody's business. There was always that one great old couple who had all the moves. They were in their eighties, but watching them dance, we knew what they were like in their teens and twenties. They were the coolest kids in town.

The next time I passed the dance studio, another couple was inside with the tight-jeaned instructor. The balding male student wore mom jeans that were belted high above his thick paunch. His partner wore a pink sweatsuit and had a short, no-fuss haircut—the kind that is now called a "Karen." They faced each other, he put one hand at her waist, she placed her hand in his, and then they began what looked like a rumba or a samba—I wasn't sure what it was called, I just knew that they were suddenly two of the sexiest people I'd seen in real life.

I had a thought then and that thought was: *Wouldn't it be fun if Denis and I took dance lessons together?* I'm the type of person who goes from having a silly little notion to a delusional obsession in a split second. As I watched the couple, I saw Denis and me at a future wedding—perhaps someday, one of our own children's wedding. I imagined the band striking up some old Frank Sinatra or Tony Bennett standard, and my eyes meeting Denis's. He'd dab his lips with his napkin, politely beg his leave from those seated around him, and make his way to me. I'd place my palm in his, and when we hit the dance floor, you'd think we were Fred Astaire and Ginger Rogers. We'd start out with a tango—gliding coolly past the stiff fox-trotters and dorky freestylers. Denis would twirl me to and fro, dip me backward, forward then—to the astonishment of all, back again over his arm into a full flip that we would improvise at that very moment. After my spritely landing, I'd wink to the crowd and Denis would do a little soft-shoe. Then—time for the surprise move we'd perfected that morning—back, back, back we'd slide in an arm-in-arm moonwalk—an homage to our generation . . . and then . . . and then . . .

I went straight home and found the dance studio's website.

"Are you looking for something to do, new and exciting with your significant other?" I was asked in a very dazzling font when I arrived at the dance school's home page. If I had to speak for both of us, the answer was, not really, we were good. There followed a list of reasons, in the same glitzy font, why ballroom dancing was not just fun, it was as essential to our longevity as wearing seat belts and having our moles checked. Dancing, I learned, is good for the heart in more ways than one.

"It's a form of fitness that involves a passionate connection with your partner!" I was already sold but I'd need something more enticing than that to convince Denis to take lessons with me. We already knew a form of fitness like that. We could do it at home, without people watching.

To my great surprise, when I suggested the classes to Denis, he was all in. Why not, he said, and I made an appointment for our first lesson.

Our instructor was the man in the tight jeans; he was a Russian man named Alex. He was probably around sixty, rather short, and quite trim. Denis later described him as "petite." When we first arrived, Alex invited us into a small office off the main studio room and launched into an unexpected sales pitch. He pointed to a large case filled with trophies he'd won as a professional dancer. He name-dropped a couple of local celebrities, one of whom is a friend of ours. These actors had hired Alex to prepare for roles in movies that required waltzing or other types of ballroom dancing. He'd taught hundreds of people to dance. He'd seen many people through state and national championships. Whatever our dance goals were, he promised, he would help us achieve them.

When I called, I was clear that we wanted to take lessons. Why the hard sell?

Denis and I sat together on a sofa, facing Alex, and it felt like we were in marriage counseling again. Alex wanted to know how he could best help us. What were our aspirations? Did we plan to move forward together in our training, or would we like solo lessons as well? If we were looking to make new friends, we'd come to the right place. There were wildly popular "mixers" every other Friday night. Everybody is welcome, everybody dances. "You get to try out new partners," Alex explained. I had no idea this Friday night "mixing" went on in our town, not to mention in our local mini mall. I glanced at Denis. He had the thousand-yard stare of a soldier being helicoptered out of 'Nam.

"We don't really go out at night," I said. "We just want to learn to dance. We don't need to learn a lot of dances. Maybe just one or two."

We paid for a few lessons, and Alex invited us out to the main room—the dance studio—for our first one. He knew that we were rank beginners, so he started with what he said was the most basic dance: the box step.

"Watch me first," he said. "I am the man, I am leading." He held his left hand out to the side, bent his right arm a short distance from his torso using the exaggerated movements of a mime.

"It's called a box step because it's like a box. The gentleman takes two steps forward, left leg first." Alex and his invisible partner moved two nimble steps forward. "Then, one step to the right."

Alex had us stand side by side with him, and we did the steps together. Then Alex told me that I, as "the lady," would be doing the steps backward. He showed me how I would take two steps back, then step to my left. We did this together, side by side.

"That's it," Alex said. "That's the basic box step. Here, Ann and I will do it together." He took my hand in his and showed us exactly where on my shoulder "the gentleman" should place his hand, and he stepped with me back, back, and to the side. Then, forward, forward, to the other side, thus closing the "box" in the box step. It was incredible; I was dancing with a partner. I was giddy with excitement.

"Good, good, good," Alex said. "Now both of you, together."

"Already?" Denis said. "Maybe you should show us again." Alex box-stepped me around the room. Then he returned me to Denis. After helping us arrange our limbs so that we were posed like dancers, Alex said, "Ready and . . . step, step, side."

I took two lively steps backward, but Denis stood like a statue, almost pulling my shoulders out of their sockets.

"What are you doing?" I hissed, staggering back toward him.

"I wasn't ready!" Denis snapped.

"No problem," said Alex. "We'll try again. Are you ready, Denis?"

"I think so," Denis said. He was suddenly drenched in sweat and was still squeezing my hand so hard I thought I felt bones crunch. He was a nervous wreck. It's strange, but Denis is very comfortable performing in front of live audiences and in front of cameras. I could never do that. Like I said, our wedding was in my mother's backyard because I think the medication for my anxiety hadn't been invented yet, and I couldn't imagine walking down a church aisle with people watching me. Now, when nobody was watching us but Alex, Denis seemed overcome with shyness.

"Honey, you need to take two steps forward," I said.

"FORWARD?" Denis shouted at Alex, who stood a few inches away. "Do I go FORWARD OR BACK?"

"The gentleman moves forward—the lady, back," Alex said. "And again . . . one, two . . ."

Denis reinforced his death grip on my hand, fixed his eye on something over my shoulder, and marched boldly across the room, forcing me to run frantically backward to keep my feet from being crushed by his. I managed to jerk him to a halt. I've ridden horses most of my life, I've stopped bolters before.

"What the hell are you doing?" I said, giving him a little shove so he'd release my sore hand.

"You almost tripped me," Denis sniped. "You need to keep your feet away from mine."

Alex said, "Denis, I'll show you how it should feel. First, I will be the gentleman."

Then, to my great astonishment, Alex took Denis in his arms and waltzed him around the room, in perfect little box steps. A lightbulb seemed to go off for Denis. "Okay, yeah!" he said.

After a few more sashays around the room, Alex told Denis it was his turn to "be the gentleman and lead." I smiled and walked toward them, my arms outstretched, but they had already waltzed off again. Alex wanted Denis to practice being the gent and leading him, not me, and Denis happily obliged. He held Alex's hand in his, placed his other hand on Alex's shoulder, and box-stepped him forward and back, side to side. He really got it! I clapped and cheered. They kept dancing. Eventually, I stopped clapping. Alex urged Denis to be more precise with his steps, Denis concentrated on this. I looked at my watch and yawned; this always happens. Everybody wants to spend more time with Denis than with me.

Finally, Alex returned my husband to me. "Now," Alex said. "Ready . . . step, step, side. Step, step, side."

Amazingly, we did a perfect box step. We did it again and again. Alex showed us how to add little turns. Then he put on some music. We stepped and sidled all over the room. We were dancing.

We took lessons with Alex every week and learned a few other steps. We learned how to swing our hips to the Latin steps. We learned how to do a few quicker "jive" steps. Every week, Alex told us we needed to practice between lessons. We promised we would, but the week would get away from us, and I always felt like I was a ten-year-old lying to my piano teacher when we lied to Alex about having practiced between lessons.

One week, our lesson was canceled due to snow. Denis and I had both put that time aside, we had nothing to do, so I thought that it might be a good time to practice. At that time, I was writing a book set in the 1920s, so I had a playlist of wonderful big band music from that era. It was the kind of music Alex played during our lessons. I synced my phone with a little speaker in our living room, but I was suddenly unsure about how to approach Denis. All I needed to do was walk into his office and suggest we practice dancing, but I felt bashful for some reason. I'd been living with Denis for over thirty years. I wouldn't have thought twice about walking naked into Denis's office and asking him to engage in any kind of sex imaginable with me right then and there. He wouldn't have thought that in the least bit odd; he'd have thought it a great idea. But dancing? It seemed weird. I finally summoned the courage and wandered into his office. When he looked up from his computer,

I said, "Hey, I was thinking, since our lesson was canceled, maybe we should—you know—practice."

Denis's face went as red as mine. "Now?" he said. His eyes darted around anxiously. "It's the middle of the afternoon." Again, we do lots of stuff in the middle of the day, stuff that involves no clothes and every kind of fun imaginable. We have this kind of fun all over the house, but now, the idea of dancing, fully clothed, in our living room, seemed beyond the realm of decent human behavior.

"Well, if you think it's a good idea," he finally said.

We made sure the doors to the house were locked and we closed the shades in our living room. What if the UPS guy showed up and saw what we were up to?

I turned on the playlist. The first song was "It Had to Be You."

Denis held out his hand, I placed my palm in his, he placed his other hand on the small of my back, and we started stepping: one, two . . . side. Back, two . . . side.

It had to be you, the song began, and we counted our steps aloud as we moved with the music.

It had to be you.

"One, two . . . side. Back, two . . . side," we counted.

I wandered around, finally found, the somebody who . . .

"One, two, side . . . back, two, side."

We box-stepped round and round the room, and as our confidence grew, we no longer counted our steps. I let Denis lead, and he held me quite gently. I'd been living with this man since I was twenty, now I was almost sixty, but it felt as if we'd just found each other for the first time.

THE GOLDEN HOUR

During our son's last year of high school, I decided to become an emergency medical technician. We lived in a town with an all-volunteer fire and ambulance service, I knew some of our town's volunteer firemen and EMTs, and I'd been encouraged to sign up. I had wanted to take the course for years, but the classes were from seven to ten in the evenings and on Saturdays. Denis was working on his series *Rescue Me*—ironically about New York City first responders—and he was often only home on weekends. I needed to make dinner for the kids and help them with homework. But now the kids drove and cooked and had homework that was too hard for me to help with, so I could finally work on becoming an EMT. I thought it would help distract me from the gnawing sadness I was feeling as my kids were getting ready to leave for college. I signed up for the monthslong course.

It was early spring when I walked into the classroom at the firehouse for the first night of EMT school. There were about fifteen other students. I wasn't the oldest person in the class; there were a couple of recently retired men and another woman about my age. The others in the class were fresh out of high school or had just finished college. Some were taking the course as part of their requirements as future state troopers or firefighters. One was in nursing school. I only mention the age differences here because it turned out to be a bit of an issue for me.

I always thought that I was okay at processing information, but after the first three-hour-long class, I realized that any aptitude I once had in this regard had almost completely deteriorated. If there were a remedial or special-ed EMT course offered, I would be in that class. I tried to nod thoughtfully when young Billy, the high school senior, asked in-depth questions regarding aortas and bile ducts, but I was dying inside. I couldn't follow anything they were talking about. Most of the class had spent at least the past twelve years learning new stuff every day. They took notes, they asked what would be on tests. I was anxious and my mind raced. I didn't know it then, but part of my problem was that I had trouble hearing—I was going deaf in one ear and had no idea, so I just whispered "What did she say?" to the person sitting next to me all the time until I realized I needed to sit in the front row.

My participation in class during those early days was limited to asking what the instructor was saying and hiding my fitful snorts and giggles whenever there was any reference made to the parts of the anatomy that involved the male reproductive system. Well, that's not entirely true. Elimination always makes me choke and nearly hyperventilate with hysterics, and the only thing that helped me gain composure was glancing at the eighteen-year-old nursing student next to me who was frowning and shaking her head.

We had a wonderfully enthusiastic head instructor named Sharon, and two veteran EMTs named Bill and Frank who taught us on weeknights and Saturdays. We had an enormous textbook and were assigned homework. Once I became more accustomed to taking it all in, I was fascinated by what I was learning. There is something almost divine about the physiology of the human body. And I mean divine very much in a spiritual sense. I'm not a religious person, but the more I learned about human organs and diseases and cures and birth and death, the heart with its arteries, veins, and the perfectly timed opening and closing valves—well, it was somehow comforting. The symbiosis is what I found most miraculous. The way the different systems of an organism work so efficiently together. I was blown away by the fact that certain cells in our bodies will rush in to help an organ that's failing, just as emergency responders will eagerly assist other members of our community who are experiencing difficulties. One night as I sat in my class, I remember looking around at my classmates with a sense of great pride. What a wonderfully diverse group. Young kids, retired people, law enforcement officers, a few moms, some future firefighters. And, of course, me. What a fine bunch. Future heroes, all of us.

This was when we were mainly focusing on how the body is supposed to work. A few weeks later, when we began focusing on what we were being trained to deal with—the body when it's malfunctioning, either due to a medical condition, trauma, or both, I began to see human physiology as some kind of cosmic joke.

What kind of bozo designs an organism whose every cell depends upon oxygen—and then decides that all the oxygen will have just one very vulnerable and narrow route into the body? I had no idea how many things can cause an airway to start closing or how flimsy the trachea is. Why isn't there an alternate access for the oxygen? I mean—just throwing this out there—gills seem to work just fine for lots of species, why not us? Or why not give one of our other orifices a second job? The anus, for example, has plenty of downtime. It really spends most of the day doing nothing; why wouldn't it have been designed to take in a little oxygen if need be?

Oh, and the femoral artery? If punctured, it becomes a blood-spurting geyser that will drain your body of its blood supply in minutes. Instead of being tucked away in some hard-to-reach place, it's at the very top of your thigh. Right in the front, where any sharp edge or pointy object can have access to it. Carotid artery? Also, very thoughtlessly located in the throat, where a knife-wielding predator or angry terrier can tear into it, and then, you know, your brain won't get any blood and you'll die. Whoever placed these arteries was apparently the same jokester who decided that babies should emerge from the most inconvenient part of the female body—a place that she cannot even see. And I'll not even go into the faulty design and lack of foresight that went into the baby head/maternal cervix size ratio.

One night, we had a nice man from the local dispatch office come to teach us about radio communications. He said it's very important for first responders to remain calm while relaying information in an emergency. One must not shout or panic, as it only makes the situation worse. As the dispatcher blithely shared an anecdote about a motor vehicle collision involving an infant and multiple traumas, I felt a rising inner hysteria. How would I be able to speak slowly using concise language in a situation like this? I'm no coolheaded, first-responder type.

I glanced around at my classmates, and instead of future heroes, I saw us in a new light—a motley assortment of feeble, jittery, know-nothings. I once left my toddler on a staircase and fled the house because a bat flew over our heads. And I'm a nervous wreck. All the time. A few weeks ago, Sharon taught us the symptoms of a panic attack, and I realized that she was describing a normal, everyday, wakeful state for me. Anxious? Sweating? Racing irrational thoughts? Check, check, check. All the time.

But I learned there are things that help a person do the right thing in emergency situations—these things are "protocols." It turns out, I love a protocol. I went to artsy schools and studied creative writing and literature. I write for a living. I've gone through life flailing about aimlessly, trying to figure out how to behave in various situations. I didn't know it, but it turns out, I'm a "rules" person. I just often don't know the rules. I really should have enlisted in the army instead of college, because having a line of command and exact protocols for every possible scenario is very comforting to me. Reckoning with the unpredictable nature of human illnesses or the mechanisms behind traumatic injuries can't always have positive outcomes, but if you arrive at a scene and follow a standard protocol, you are less likely to panic. You do things in order. There's a system; there are people superior to you who will take charge. I listened to our instructors talk about their encounters with lives teetering on the brink, and I learned how it's possible to keep a person in danger from tumbling over the edge—to keep them with us, by treating, shocking, comforting, oxygenating, stabilizing, keeping the systems running, on the scene and all the way to the hospital. I learned about the importance of efficiency because time is always running out when there is severe trauma or illness.

Before I took my EMT training course, I had only heard the term "golden hour" as it's used in filmmaking. In cinematography and photography, the golden hour is the first hour after dawn or the last hour before dusk when the light becomes very fine. It has to do with the sun being so low on the horizon that it casts long shadows. There is some kind of filtering effect that adds colorful qualities and tinted hues. The evening "golden hour" often culminates in a beautiful sunset, but even when it doesn't, there's usually a very rare atmosphere that makes everything look a little better. Filmmakers will spend hours, sometimes days preparing cameras, equipment, and actors for a scene that calls for the "golden hour." I've always loved the term, it's beautiful to me, there's something magical about it. Denis and I will sometimes just say it, if we're on the beach at the right moment or the light is hitting a building in an old city late in the day: "It's the golden hour."

During EMT training, I learned of the medical meaning of the "golden hour," which is what prehospital emergency care is all about. Dr. R. Adams Cowley, an American military physician and one of the pioneers of our modern EMS services, wrote, "There is a golden hour between life and death. If you are critically injured, you have less than sixty minutes to survive. You might not die right then; it may be three days or two weeks later—but something has happened in your body that is irreparable."

The golden hour in medicine, as in photography, is not meant to be taken too literally, it may be more or less than an hour, but the idea, is that the early moments after a trauma or medical event is a very precious time.

It was during World War I that French military surgeons became aware of the "golden hour" concept of caring for trauma victims on battlefields. Prior to that, injured soldiers and civilians were carried or otherwise transported to medical units or hospitals for treatment. Later, during the Vietnam War, having medical personnel treat trauma victims in the field rather than just patch them up and transport them to the closest hospital became standard protocol. In fact, practices of the military field medics in the Vietnam War were the model upon which the modern American prehospital emergency care system was developed.

As recently as the 1960s, ambulances were basically just vehicles that were used to transport patients to the hospital. The drivers usually had no medical training. In fact, they were often undertakers. Since hearses were sometimes the only vehicles in a community that could accommodate a person lying flat, many undertakers moonlighted by picking up the sick and injured and driving them to the hospital.

I assumed that once I became a certified EMT, I would be able to save a person when called to the scene of a cardiac arrest. In fact, by the time an EMT or medic arrives, it's usually too late. I was taught that it was unlikely I would ever save somebody's life by performing CPR as an EMT, but I had a very good chance of saving somebody's life performing CPR as a Good Samaritan—that is, as a person who happens to be there when another has a heart attack. That's why everybody should know CPR. It's those golden minutes that make all the difference.

A few things I had learned by month two of my EMT training:

> The heart really is a lonely hunter. It's the only organ that has "automaticity"—the ability to generate an impulse on its own. It doesn't need another organ or hormone or nerve to start it up. It's self-generating. I didn't know that. It's a rather basic form of plumbing equipment designed to pump fluid. There are some important valves, nodes, chambers, and pipes, all in a sleek, ever-pulsing container. Yet it's full of electricity and has built-in pacemakers.
>
> The reason a person's skin becomes cool or cold when they are in shock is because the body decides to focus all its energy on heating and sustaining the body's core, where the vital organs are. The blood, which is necessary for proper oxygenation or perfusion of all the organs, sort of

tells the skin to fend for itself, and rushes in to offer help where it's really needed.

Women often don't experience chest pain when having a heart attack. They commonly report that they "just don't feel right." Unusual fatigue for a number of days is a red flag for women that they might be having heart trouble.

Television dramas such as *ER* have given the public an unrealistic faith in the AED (defibrillator) devices that EMTs use when somebody has had a cardiac arrest. As soon as the family members see the machine come out, they all breathe a sigh of relief and start making all sorts of plans for their nonbreathing, nonresponsive loved one. When the AED fails to revive a patient, as it sometimes does, the family and friends are unable to believe it. When a person goes into cardiac arrest and loses their pulse, they need the AED immediately. By the time the first responders show up, it's usually too late.

The criteria a person must meet in order to be pronounced dead by an EMT is morbidly funny. Only doctors, medical examiners, or coroners can pronounce a person dead. A person with a basic EMT certification is able to make a decision not to resuscitate a person and presume them dead only if they are missing their entire head, have been flattened as thin as a pancake, or have no more flesh attached to their skeleton. Otherwise, somebody else makes the call.

EMTs are taught to protect the dignity and integrity of a patient and his or her family, whether the patient is living or dead.

Professional EMTs and paramedics, whether paid or volunteer, are extraordinary people. Our teachers were amazing. They love what they do. They do it out of love.

It was a hot summer day when I parked my car in front of the large Hartford office building. Inside, I was met by a receptionist who handed me a list of test regulations. I was photographed and fingerprinted. Then I was led into an interior chamber where I was fingerprinted again, and all my personal belongings (except for my clothes) were stored in a locker.

It was time. I was about to take the National Registry of Emergency Medical Technicians cognitive test. This was the last of the tests that I would need to take to become a certified emergency medical technician. I had spent months in a classroom and on practice ambulance rides with seasoned crews, now my knowledge was being put to the test. I was told there would be seventy to a hundred and forty questions, and that there would be two hours to take the test. The test was taken in a room filled with cubicles. Each cubicle had a computer. I was led to my assigned computer and an instructor showed me how to log in.

I began the test. I was introduced, one by one, to a very interesting but easily the most depressing cast of characters I've ever encountered. I signed an agreement at the testing site that I wouldn't share details of the test, so I can't be specific, but there were disoriented diabetics who seemed to be drunk, toddlers who couldn't breathe, violent drug addicts, injured cyclists, and old people clutching their chests. My job was to not be distracted by the confusing wrong answers to the questions about each patient, but instead, to pick the right answer.

The trickiest questions for me involved mass-casualty scenarios where patients must be triaged. This might be a train wreck or mass-shooting situation. When faced with multiple casualties, first responders must determine whose life is most precarious, who must be treated and transported first, and who can wait. Most ambulances have mass-casualty incident kits. The MCI kits have color-coded tags that are attached to each patient. The tags are green, yellow, red, and black. Green tags are attached to the walking wounded—people with minor scrapes and abrasions. Red tags are for the most urgent cases—those who need to be first in the ambulances. Black tags are for dead folk.

Yellow is the secondary urgent care group after red, and this can be a tricky call. A yellow might be a young man with a broken arm and minor abrasions but no uncontrolled bleeding. It can also be an unconscious man with second- and third-degree burns over

80 percent of his body, with poor vitals. It depends on who else is injured and what your available resources are. If it's an incident with many casualties and one ambulance on scene, the burned, failing respiratory man is sadly a yellow, not a red. His condition is so severe that he is likely to die, no matter how soon he's transported, so a person with a higher probability of survival will go before him.

Our instructors had warned us to beware of the screaming toddler—both in practice and on this test. She's crying so hard, poor baby, with abrasions and a deformed arm. It's human nature to rush her to the ambulance first, but she's not a red. Her crying indicates a good airway, her fast breathing and heart rate are from fear and pain. She'll survive with delayed treatment. She might be a yellow or even a red in some mass-casualty situations. In my test, she was in an accident with two people with traumatic brain injuries and a pregnant woman, but only one ambulance on scene. Baby girl was a green. She could be treated, the arm could be immobilized, but she'd have to wait for the next ambulance.

The test took about an hour. The next day I got an email from my EMS instructor, Sharon. I had passed! I was now a nationally registered emergency medical technician.

I'd been an EMT for two years when our daughter, Devin, was a freshman in college. I missed her, but she was only an hour away, so I visited often. One October Saturday we spent the afternoon in Sleepy Hollow. The town of Sleepy Hollow was originally part of Tarrytown—a lovely village on the Hudson River, just about a half hour north of Manhattan in Westchester County, New York. Sleepy Hollow was made famous by Washington Irving, who wrote the story of poor Ichabod Crane and his terrifying flight from the ghost of the Headless Horseman in *The Legend of Sleepy Hollow*, first published in 1820. Dev was a photographer for her college newspaper and was sent there on assignment. We spent the afternoon poking around the village and then we wandered into the town's famous cemetery.

The Sleepy Hollow Cemetery is enormous and old and is spread along a series of grassy hills that offer magnificent views of the distant hills. It was late in the afternoon when we found the place and started wandering amid the tombstones and statues and dollhouse-like crypts that cast long shadows across the quiet paths. At first we furtively glanced at the headstones as we walked along. It felt wrong to stop and stare—it felt like walking along a street lined with great old houses and just glancing at the windows because, even though you're curious, you don't want the occupants to think you're snooping. It took us a little while before we felt comfortable enough to really stop and look at the epitaphs and the lovely carvings and statues. They were designed to be admired, we realized. By people like us.

There were so many species of trees planted there that it seemed like a delightful arboretum strewn with headstones. The leaves were all just starting to brighten from that dull, flat wall of summer green into their various brilliant tones of autumn. It had been hot that week, but now it was growing chilly. The light was that thin, yellow October light that made me think of my childhood; of pumpkins and piles of crispy dead leaves; ghosts, itchy leggings, and mittens. It smelled like somebody was burning leaves—a practice that I thought had been outlawed everywhere. It smelled like a place where I had never lived but always imagined, like a neighbor's home that my family used to drive past and see all lit up in the dusk—the dad out burning leaves, the mom, I imagined, baking pies. Fall is a very nostalgic time for me; it fills me with vague memories of strangers' imaginary childhoods. And my own childhood too, my own rubber boots, pumpkins, mittens, my own young parents and my little sister and big brother. The piles of leaves, our sweet tabby cat who, as Halloween approached, seemed bewitched and conniving. Our hot costumes and trick-or-treat bags that were old pillowcases. Trying to breathe through a tiny mouth hole in a mask from Woolworth's; trying to see through the crooked eyes. It was so hard to breathe and see when we were out trick-or-treating on Halloween, we were just so utterly thrilled with fright and greed.

That chilly autumn afternoon with Devin, the sun was setting at an angle that lit the western faces of all the tombstones. When we touched their surfaces, they warmed our hands like stones that had been heated in an oven. Sleepy Hollow Cemetery is an inviting place. I know it sounds odd—who wants to feel welcome or invited to a cemetery?—but it felt like a lovely place to retire. For eternity.

I'd been out on several urgent ambulance calls during recent weeks, calls involving a couple of ninetysomethings, and I'd been thinking a lot about the way people's lives come to an end. For some, it might be after a ride in the back of an ambulance. The heat is usually on because the patient is in shock or not able to be properly clothed due to various intravenous lines, so it's warm. There's only a small window in the back, so when we're speeding along the highway, there's almost a sense of flight—we could be in a jet or a rocket, only the jostling and occasional sharp turns remind us that we're still on earth. The ambulance, just a few months before, had been a little scary to me, but now, it was as familiar as my own car. I didn't notice all the lights and equipment anymore. Now I could focus on the patients.

If they were conscious, those we treated and transported usually tried to hide their fear. We EMTs tried to make it a little better. We'd joke about the bad driving of the chief and tell the patient her ride home from the hospital would be a lot more comfortable.

We wanted each passenger to believe they'd be going home, that this wasn't their last ride; that our strange, sleepy, unwashed faces weren't the last faces they'd ever see, but just in case they were, we tried to look like we weren't afraid for them. We did this when people were conscious, semiconscious, or completely unresponsive, because who knew what they could and couldn't hear.

We upped their oxygen; we rechecked their vitals. We told them that they were fine, that they weren't alone, that there was nothing to worry about, that we were almost there.

MY LIFE IN DOGS

I wasn't raised by wolves, but I was taught to walk by an Irish setter named Brendan. Brendan ran away when I was around three years old, so I only have photos and family stories by which to remember him. In one photo, Brendan is sitting and I'm standing with my adoring face turned up to him as if he were the sun. His head is about two feet higher than mine. I'm wearing a little dress, anklet socks, and Mary Janes. Brendan is wearing a roguish grin and a stunning coat, which I know was a deep red color although the photo is black and white.

From what I'm told, Brendan loved everybody, was great with small children, and was by far the best-looking member of our family, but he was also a scoundrel, an escape artist, and a thief. The two things I grew up knowing about him were that I learned to walk by clutching his fur and pulling myself to my feet. He gently supported me as I took my first steps, then he stayed close to "spot" me when I let go of him and toddled alone. The other legend of Brendan was that he stole a mailman's bag, full of mail, which he proudly brought home and which my father either did or did not bury in our backyard, depending upon whom you ask.

When Brendan was training me to walk, he was gentle and moved slowly. The rest of the time he was a red tornado of destruction. We lived in Wayne, Pennsylvania, then, in a small house with a backyard surrounded by a six-foot-high fence. Brendan would soar over the fence like a bird, then he'd be gone for a few hours or a few days, but he'd eventually either come home, or the person he'd taken up with would call my mother to say that they had Brendan.

We lived near an estate area—an old-moneyed, mainline Philadelphia suburb. Brendan was drawn to regal, aristocratic types like himself, so he'd streak over to the "right" part of town and try to insinuate himself into high society by crashing catered cocktail parties, lounging like a movie star on pool settees, or exercising children's terrified ponies around their paddocks.

Irish setters were originally bred as gun dogs, but they're more independent than retrievers. When hunting, they cover large amounts of territory, not always at the hunter's side, and when they locate a quail or pheasant, they "set," or lie down facing the bird, so that the hunter may flush out the bird and safely shoot over them. In a city or suburban setting, these hardwired hunting and roaming traits are less than ideal. Brendan sailed over our fence one final day, when my mother was in the hospital having my sister, Meg, but this time, he didn't come home. My mother was devastated.

Our next dog was Coco, a shepherd-mix puppy who came to us when we lived in Annapolis. She was allowed to run loose when we moved from downtown Annapolis to a leafy suburb. We children ran loose; our dogs ran loose. I was only six when we left Maryland, but my memories of both neighborhoods in Maryland are like *Peanuts* cartoons. There were no grown-ups. We children roamed the woods, streams, and rural roads in grimy little packs. It was great fun and Coco was always bounding along with us.

When we moved to Midland, Michigan, it was a different type of neighborhood. There were no woods, no fields. Coco had to be walked on a leash, which she wasn't used to doing. She was too big and strong for us kids; my mother and father were very busy. My mother found Coco a "nice home on a farm." She swears to this day she really did find her a home on a farm.

On my seventh birthday, I was given my first dog of my own—a miniature poodle puppy named Beau, who lived until I was an adult. I taught him many tricks. I was in charge of his care when I was only seven, so he developed some bad tricks of his own, which included snapping at people, humping everyone and everything (and trying to bite those who rebuffed him). I was about ten years old when we got Gus, a shepherd/collie mix puppy who also lived until I was in college.

When I met Denis in Boston, I was a junior in college and I had just adopted an adorable puppy named Brett. She was a sweet mutt; Denis and I adored her. She was very smart. She walked all over Boston with me without a leash. She stopped at curbs and waited until I said okay before she crossed. She waited outside our local coffee shop for me. She embarrassingly stopped at our neighborhood liquor store whenever we passed—I was a regular customer and I always bought her a beef jerky when I bought my goods. Later, she attended AA meetings with me.

People tend to have a "type" when it comes to dogs. Because of Brett, who was a shaggy, black terrier mix, scruffy terrier mixes became our type. When our children were little and we lived in Manhattan, we adopted Pongo, and about a year later, Rocky—two rescues who were the same adorable combination of terrier and other unknown wiry-coated breeds. They looked so alike, and were so cute, that people often asked us what breed they were. I got tired of having to explain that they weren't related, they didn't even come from the same state, so I invented a breed and told everybody who asked that they were Galway terriers. There is no recognized breed called a Galway terrier as far as I know, but many people said things like, "My aunt bred Galways!" Or "I love Galway terriers!"

We moved to the country with our two children, Pongo and Rocky, and soon we added two Irish wolfhounds to the family. This was our first experience buying a puppy from a breeder, and she was a very responsible breeder. She carefully vetted us before agreeing to allow us to purchase a puppy. We ended up taking two because Denis worried that if we had just one, he'd feel like a freak—Irish wolfhounds are the tallest canine breed. Clancy and Duffy were very goofy puppies. Irish wolfhounds are, in my mind, the perfect protection dogs. Everybody who came to our house was able to see their great size. We had an enormous dog door for them that an adult human could climb through, but they are shy and rarely aggressive, so there's little chance of them harming anyone. I always knew a stranger was approaching our house. Instead of barking, the wolfhounds would tiptoe into my office and peer anxiously out the window from behind my chair. The downside is that, like all giant breeds, Irish wolfhounds have short lives. Duffy died at a young age of bloat—a serious stomach condition common with that breed. Clancy lived to be almost nine years old, which is very old for an Irish wolfhound. At some point we added Daphne, a Lab/poodle mix, who was, in my mind, as close to perfect as a dog can be. Then we adopted Lulu, who was a Hurricane Katrina rescue. Lulu, according to her DNA panel, was half St. Bernard, one quarter Rhodesian ridgeback, and one quarter Airedale, and that seemed exactly right. She was very large, her paws were like baseball mitts, they were huge in relation to the rest of her body, which was also very large. I think the outsized paws and generally goofball disposition caused the rescue organization to age her as a puppy who was six to nine months old. She behaved like a puppy, and they thought she might grow into those paws. Our vet thought she was between one and two years old when we adopted her.

At first, we thought Lulu's boundless enthusiasm was unmitigated joy and gratitude at her changed circumstances. She was thrilled to find herself on a small farm instead of on death row. We noticed early on that she had on-and-off lameness in her hind end, and our vet diagnosed her with double hip dysplasia. This was our second rescue dog who required hip surgery that cost many thousands of dollars, and she wouldn't be our last.

Lulu was just about the sweetest creature I've ever known,

but she suffered from what appeared to be a staggeringly low IQ. We wondered whether she suffered some sort of brain damage as a puppy or was inbred or something. She possessed no problem-solving skills. None. Most carnivorous mammals have some problem-solving skills because hunting for flighty prey requires strategy. Wild dogs must communicate with each other to hunt in packs, and that is why dogs make such great human companions. They've learned to interpret our movements and much of our language, and through repetition, can be taught to do many useful things, such as coming when they're called, or getting off the bed when told. This is the ordinary dog I'm talking about. Lulu was no ordinary dog.

The time she dove into the dishwasher to lick a plate and backed up with the entire bottom rack of dishes attached to her collar, we laughed until we wept. She was so large that she was able to run around our house with a dishwasher rack attached to her collar. She was still madly licking the dishes as she dragged the rack from room to room, smashing dishes everywhere. When she wore a chair as a necklace, in another act of outrageous greed during a holiday dinner, we were, again, howling with laughter.

But here's something that wasn't so funny: She didn't understand the "come" command (or really, any human words). She wasn't being stubborn when she didn't come when called. It's just something she couldn't figure out. On a cold, snowy night, she would sit on our hill, staring dolefully down at the house. I'd open the door and call her. She'd whine and squirm and do all sorts of theatrics, but the dog would not come. I'd shake a box of treats and make her mad with desire. She'd yelp and bark. If only she could be there with me—in the warm house, with all the food—but she couldn't figure out how to make that happen. Each time, I had to don a coat and boots, walk up to her, and when I reached her side, she leapt joyfully and covered me with kisses for saving her, and then we ran down to the house together. The next night, when I called her, she was stumped all over again.

We had four dogs for many years: Lulu; Daphne; Holly, a small terrier/dachshund rescue who is now fourteen and still very healthy and active; and Gomer, a gorgeous, sweet Leonberger. Gomer was given to us by friends who were unable to keep him because they were moving. Gomer was about 125 pounds and died at age seven of bone cancer, which is sadly common in larger breeds, especially if they're spayed or neutered too early.

Currently we have three dogs—Holly, Bowie, and Eddie.

We decided to get Bowie, our poodle, from a breeder because we'd had the rescue dogs with hip dysplasia, and we had just lost a second dog to bone cancer. This time we wanted a dog whose parents had been tested for genetic diseases.

I have always wanted a standard poodle—it probably had to do with the fact that my first dog of my own was a poodle. Our poodle looks like a large Labradoodle because we don't have him clipped like a poodle. But his parents and grandparents had clear health records and he is now seven and is very healthy. When we got Bowie, our only other dog was little Holly. Our kids were grown, and we were moving to a smaller house and property. We had been a four-dog family for quite a while, but now we wanted to be a two-dog family. Around the time we got Bowie, our daughter, Devin, adopted a cute, wiry terrier mix to live with her in Manhattan. Eddie looked a bit like her childhood dogs, Rocky and Pongo. Eddie came from a rescue that brought dogs to New England from Texas. Eddie was about four or five months old when she adopted him. Her job allowed employees to bring their dogs to work.

Eddie wasn't cut out for the city. He was reactive and fearful. He was very hyperactive, and I thought there was something feral about him. We took care of him when she was traveling, and I'm going to be honest, I didn't like this dog. He was cute in his puppy pictures because he has a scruffy face and enormous upright ears, but he had the body and coat of a coyote, and he moved like a coyote—his head carried low, and sort of slinking. I looked out my window one day and saw a coyote approaching our little dog Holly in a predatorial crouch-walk and I screamed until I realized it was just Eddie.

Eddie stared at me all the time. Most dogs don't like prolonged eye contact with one another or with humans. Eddie followed me around the house, and whenever I glanced at him, he was boring holes in my eyes with his. He was a little creepy in that way, but he was also, by far, the most intelligent dog I had ever known, and this, along with his appearance, made me certain that he was part coyote. Wolves and coyotes are more intelligent than domestic dogs, and it is rare, but domestic dogs and coyotes do breed. Eddie was making Devin's life miserable. He was becoming more and more anxious on city streets, and more reactive toward people, barking and snarling when people tried to pet him. He slipped his harness once, when something frightened him, and ran into a busy city street. Devin refused to give up on him, but she was a young woman in the city, and she couldn't enjoy her dog. Her anxious dog kept her from enjoying much else.

Eddie came to stay with us for a week, and I decided to have our vet do a DNA panel on him. I hadn't told Devin, but I really was convinced he was part coyote. When Denis asked what I would do if he turned out to be a coy-dog, I said, "We can send him to a coyote wildlife sanctuary, where he belongs." As I said, I really didn't like Eddie. His "bark" was a high-pitched scream when he was excited or anxious. He used this banshee shriek to ward off anybody who came near him, both inside our house and out. He was highly neurotic and was making Bowie, who was the exact same adolescent age, also a little edgy.

When the DNA results came back, we learned that Eddie is a domestic dog, not a coyote hybrid. But we were quite surprised by his breed makeup. Eddie is 50 percent Australian cattle dog (AKA blue heeler), meaning one of his parents was likely a purebred cattle dog. The other parent completed the toxic brew of pit bull, husky, and Chihuahua which is our Eddie. I hadn't suspected that Eddie was partially a herding breed, but now his genius-level intelligence, the staring, the hypervigilant behavior made sense. A herding dog who can herd livestock or engage in other mind-engaging, physically demanding work all day is a wonderful dog. A cattle dog who moves from Texas to Manhattan might fare well, but Eddie is naturally timid and weak-nerved, and city life was a nightmare for him.

Eddie was happier in the country with us. He clearly wasn't going to be a happy city dog, so I told Devin that I would work with Eddie a little bit—maybe train him to be more obedient and teach him some cute tricks, and hopefully, that would help us find him a more suitable home. I did not want this dog.

I've always loved training dogs and horses. I learned about "clicker training" in the 1990s. It's a type of positive-reinforcement training that has become standard for training everything from pets to Seeing Eye dogs and police/military K-9 dogs. Clicker or "marker" training was first used in training marine mammals in places like Sea World. Because the dolphins and orcas were doing their behaviors in the water, and their trainers were standing poolside, there was no way to immediately praise or reward a behavior the instant it happened, the way one might do with a puppy who sits on command. Whistles were used to "mark" the appropriate behavior. A dolphin jumps out of the water, the trainer marks it with a whistle, and the dolphin swims over for its fish reward. Clickers or marker words (I say "Yes!" when our dogs do the right thing. For horses, I use a clicking sound with my tongue) tell the animal that the thing they just did that instant was the right thing. The dogs and horses I've worked with love this kind of engagement training, and I do too.

Eddie not only watches TV, he seems to follow some of the plots. He remembers characters in series, but he isn't great at discerning who's the good guy and who's the villain. One winter I watched the series *Breaking Bad*. At the end of the pilot episode (SPOILER AHEAD!), Walter White points a pistol at the camera.

Eddie always reacts by scream-barking and hurling himself at the TV whenever he sees a gun, but seeing the gun pointed at us made him attack it with more than his usual ferocity. After that, he growled whenever he saw Walter White. Some would say that's proof he's a good judge of character. But at some point, he saw a character named Tuco cooking food, and from that moment on, Eddie's tail wagged with glee whenever he saw Tuco. He'd sniff the air and lick his chops every time Tuco was on camera. Tuco was a psychopath. Eddie thought he was a saint, and he almost destroyed the TV when Tuco was killed.

I never noticed how many dogs there are in television commercials until Eddie came into our lives. If he sees a golden retriever in a laxative commercial, it is branded in his memory forever. If he's in the kitchen with me and he hears the first notes of that commercial's jingle, coming from the TV in the living room, he races to that room, stands before the TV with his hackles up, and waits for the dog at the end. He has memorized countless jingles. Recognizing a piece of music involves understanding and memorizing distinct sound patterns. I didn't know, until Eddie, that nonhuman mammals are capable of this kind of decoding.

I've had dogs who liked toys and treats as rewards. Eddie is obsessed with toys and treats, but his joy comes not from the reward but from manipulating me into surrendering the reward to him. If I pick up a ball, Eddie loses his mind—he barks, spins, leaps in the air. If I throw the ball, he might run after it once, but if I throw it again, he looks at me as if to say, *Well, now I have to go all the way over there and get it again; I thought we were going to have fun*. If dogs could shrug their shoulders or say, *What the fuck are you doing?* Eddie would do those things every time I threw a ball for him.

One day, when I was still getting to know him, I was holding the ball and he was leaping and shrieking his head off. Then I said, "Sit," a command he knew. He sat and I tossed the ball. He caught it in midair and dropped it at my feet, staring at me with his tail wagging furiously. I asked him to sit again, and said "Yes!" and tossed the ball. Again, he shot through the air, caught it, and returned it to me. I started teaching him other commands—down, stay, go to a chair, get on the chair and wait—and each thing he did was rewarded with the ball toss. Eddie was transformed. I had never seen Eddie show joy—something I was used to seeing dogs express. Now he was grinning, his tail was wagging, he was thrilled. I brought home some dog Frisbees, and then Eddie's joy knew no bounds. I watched videos of competitive disk dogs. It took me about five minutes to teach Eddie to back up when asked, and to go around me when I was about to send the Frisbee out. I taught him to jump over my shoulders when I knelt, and he taught himself to do a backflip if I tossed a Frisbee over his head while he stood facing me.

I was starting to fantasize about our future world disk champion title when Eddie started limping. It turned out that Eddie had severe dysplasia in both elbows. By this time, I was in love with Eddie. His surgery cost us thousands of dollars. I was able to spend many weeks doing rehab exercises with him, something I wouldn't have been able to do when I had kids at home or worked outside the home. Even with the surgery, he will have premature arthritis in the elbows.

I had wanted to do agility and disk-training competitions with him, but he's not supposed to jump. Instead, Eddie has learned great obedience skills and countless tricks. He heels, his shoulder almost touching my calf, backward, forward, sideways. When I stop, he sits, his eyes riveted on my face.

I thought I knew a lot about dogs, but Eddie has taught me more. He's taught me about emotions that all mammals share. He's taught me about our need for love, motivation, and the importance of honesty and clarity when communicating with others—especially when communicating with animals. He reminds me to try much harder to look at things from the perspective of others. He's taught me to be more patient. Eddie is my familiar—the things I didn't like about him were the things that I don't like about me. I'm anxious and fearful in social situations. I can't chill; I fret about things to come.

I have many videos of Eddie on Instagram and Facebook. His heeling skills, combined with tricks such as weaving between my legs as I walk, scooting backward, crawling, and walking upright for long periods of time, make him appear to be dancing with me when I add music. I used to have to hold a ball when he was engaged in these tricks. Now, he drops the ball and has no interest in it until he's done the weaving or spinning that I request. When I release him with a "Yes!" he pounces on the ball with immense joy. It looks like I've taught Eddie to do behaviors that I reward with the ball. It looks like I've taught him restraint by leaving the ball where he can get it and having his attention on me when I ask him to do something. It looks like I have a great degree of control over my dog.

In fact, Eddie is convinced that he is in complete control of me, which as a herding dog, brings him great joy. He wants the ball, but he doesn't just want me to throw it. He wants to sort out what to do with his body to get me to release the ball. He likes to control me, he likes to control everything, he likes to organize. One of the earliest tricks I taught him was to pick up his toys and put them in a basket. He caught on instantly. Soon I had him removing clothing from the dryer and putting it in a basket. One day I saw a video of a dog who placed plastic bowls of varying sizes inside the other bowls. Kind of like Russian dolls—the largest first, then the medium bowl goes inside that one, then the smallest. It took less than ten minutes for Eddie to figure that out. It took even less time to teach him his favorite indoor activities—finding my phone or finding my keys. He'd love to spend every day of his life racing around our house, sniffing under furniture, tossing cushions off sofas in his search for whatever I've sent him to find. He's a dog—his nose makes finding very easy.

I've read a lot about dog behavior. Several years ago, there was a lot of whining among my Facebook friends about a study purporting that our dogs don't like it when we hug them. On a *Psychology Today* blog, Dr. Stanley Coren explained that while it's scientific fact that hugging dogs reduces stress-levels in humans, this appears to be a one-way street. He cited a now-famous study in which animal behaviorists analyzed photos of humans hugging their canines. The humans in the pictures exhibit facial characteristics that, according to scientists, indicate they are experiencing something commonly called "joy." When humans are happy, we tend to curl our lips up at the corners. Often, we show our teeth. In the photos that were studied, in addition to the lip curling, the humans' eyes are sometimes wide enough to reveal the white portions. In other photos, they have closed their eyes entirely, another sign of human joy. Their dogs' faces, however, in photo after photo, showed widened eyes and flattened ears. These are often signs of canine disgust and potential aggression.

Reactions on my Facebook feed were mixed. Some people expressed remorse for being so selfish. Was there any way to reverse the trauma they had unwittingly caused their best friend? Others talked about the sense of entitlement that dogs have today. We feed them, we walk them, we pick up their feces, yet we aren't allowed to hug them? It violates their "boundaries"?

"It was always good for me," Denis said, when I read him the study. "I thought it must be good for her too."

"Well, it's not," I said, leaning over to comfort our dog Daphne without touching her. I praised her with my eyes. I soothed her with my thoughts. It worked—she showed no signs of stress or aggression, she just continued to sleep.

I've always understood that our dogs merely tolerate our hugs, that they don't love them. But then, I don't love it when they tongue-kiss my mouth or hump my leg. I took it for granted that we compromise, that there's a little give-and-take in any relationship.

This study made me question everything about my bond with our dogs. Were they trying to inhibit a bite urge every time we hugged? Why didn't they run away? Is it a form of Stockholm syndrome, this willingness on their part to undergo torture? Within days of the *Psychology Today* piece, behaviorists were citing conflicting studies that indicate our dogs might be okay with hugs. Some dogs might even like them. If it makes you feel good, go ahead and hug, is where the dog-science community now sits (and hopefully stays).

Well, not so fast, dog experts. How were we supposed to go back to where we once were? I wasn't going to force myself on my dogs. No means no.

I decided to look at some photos of our dog Gomer, who'd died several months before. Gomer was a big, beautiful, immensely huggable dog. He wasn't just handsome. He was extraordinarily kind, patient, and forgiving. He had a great sense of humor. He liked to carry our guests' underwear around the house—that joke never got old with him. Sometimes he'd carry my own unmentionables out through the dog door and display them on our front lawn. He was a foodie, like most dogs, but his favorite food was toast. He'd rather have toast than beef tenderloin. He weighed 125 pounds, but he allowed our tiny terrier to pretend she was the boss of him. He kept up this pretense all his life. He was the kind of dog that humans want to hug with their entire bodies. I hugged this dog every day. Some of these hugs were captured in photos. In some of the photos he seems quite comfortable, but in others, I now see what the behaviorists were talking about. In those photos, I'm smiling, but Gomer looks tense. Apprehensive.

But how can we know exactly what our dogs are really feeling? If they're stressed, how do we know that hugs are the cause and not something else? Dogs have keener senses—they hear better than we do, they can smell fear, predict earthquakes, detect cancerous tumors in humans. They have internal clocks (but theirs are always set seven years ahead of ours).

So the angst they feel when we hug them, what if it's about something we tune out most of the time but they cannot? What if it's a mournful, preternatural understanding that hugs—like walks, toast, naps, everything good in this world—will all be over some day, and whenever that day comes, it will be forever and far too soon.

ON BEING NICE

Somebody once told me that you can learn everything you need to know about another person on the tennis court, and this is true, in my experience. No matter how one might try to behave on the court—kindness, cruelty, generosity, and dishonesty come out in the heat of a match, especially when playing doubles.

I play tennis with some wonderful people, but I also know a few seemingly nice people who turn into borderline sociopaths the minute they set foot on the court. A woman I'll call "Leslie" is a perfect example of this Jekyll-and-Hyde phenomenon.

Off court, Leslie's a perky, blond, former cheerleader type. Her tennis skort, top, and sneakers are always color-coordinated, and she is somehow able to wear mascara that never smears all over her face when she perspires. Off court, Leslie not only remembers the other tennis players' names, Leslie also remembers our children's names, and is the first to post Happy Birthday on our Facebook pages.

But the minute she steps onto a tennis court, Leslie morphs into a loudmouth, a bully, a cheater, and most annoyingly, a chronic other-blamer. Her doubles partners are always the reason she loses. Her brilliant strategizing is the reason she and her partners earn a rare win.

Leslie was my partner in a recent match, during which she constantly berated me, because she thinks that's helpful. We lost.

"YOU HIT IT TOO HARD!" she yelled whenever my ball went out, in case I didn't understand basic physics.

"THAT'S MINE!" she shrieked in the middle of one of my volleys, distracting everybody on the court, including me.

"THAT WAS YOURS!" she yelled when she swung and missed a ball that had practically landed in her racket.

"Out!" she always says, when an opponent's ball lands an inch or two inside the baseline. When challenged, she cites the USTA rule about line calls.

"IT'S MY CALL!" she snaps when an opponent suggests that she might not have clearly seen where the ball landed.

"But it was inside the—" says her opponent.

"MY CALL!"

What I find most galling is that Leslie is one of the few people in our group who is a worse tennis player than I am, but she offers me free tennis lessons whenever we play together. She coached me, over the course of that match, about how I needed to change my grip, my position at the net, my attitude, my body mass index, and my brand of deodorant. During the final set, she served a ball into the back of my head and then yelled at me for being in the way of her serve. I apologized for standing where one stands when a partner is serving. Fortunately, her serves are so soft, it wasn't painful.

In fact, my first thought was that a moth had briefly alighted on my scalp.

After that match, my friend Kate walked back to the parking lot with me. Kate had been on the opposite side of the court—the winning side—so I asked her if she'd witnessed the various human rights atrocities that Leslie had committed against me. I told Kate how rude and inconsiderate Leslie had been, and what an outrageous cheater she is with her sketchy line calls and dodgy scorekeeping. I had Leslie's number the minute I met her, I told Kate, I saw right through her saccharine charm; I know an insufferable bully when I see one (but instead of "bully," I might have used the C-word).

I was angry at Leslie, but I was even more furious at myself. As usual, I'd responded to all her unsportsmanlike behavior with gritted teeth and a stony silence. I'd recently come to the realization that Leslie's bossiness was at its worst when I was her partner. I tolerated her behavior because I hate confrontations. Others would call Leslie out on her bullshit, but I was too much of a wimp.

I was in the middle of sharing this insight about my Christ-like suffering at the hands of the devil when Kate elbowed and shushed me because the devil herself was flouncing past us toward her car.

"Bye, Leslie," we called to her brightly.

"Bye, my girlfriends!" she replied with a gleaming smile and what she thought was a sassy little wink. Her mascara was still annoyingly only on her eyelashes.

"Bye, my *girlfriends*," I mimicked when she was out of earshot, then I continued my inventory of her faults. "I mean, her breast implants take up the whole court, how the hell am I supposed to stay out of her way? Did you see when she tripped me? I ended up with my face buried in her bosom."

Kate expressed her sorrow at having missed that.

I stewed a bit more, silently chiding myself again for not standing up to Leslie.

"You know, Kate," I said grimly. "The problem with me is—I'm too nice."

At this, Kate stopped moving. She grabbed my wrist to steady herself because she was seizing with laughter and couldn't walk. I watched her gasp for air, tears streaming down her cheeks. I looked around to see what had caused this hysteria. Had Leslie slipped on a banana peel? Had her hair extensions come loose and fluttered off with the wind? No, Leslie was nowhere in sight.

"What's so funny?" I asked.

Kate looked surprised. She immediately tried to stifle her laughter and appear serious, then she collapsed with giggles. She attempted a straight face again, but then snorted laughter out of her nose.

I tried to match her mood with a quizzical smile. "What is it?" I pressed.

"I'm sorry," Kate finally managed. "I thought . . . you know . . . that you were making a joke."

I frowned as I recalled the words that she'd thought had been a joke: *The problem with me is—I'm too nice.*

"Wait," I said. "So you mean . . . am I to understand that . . . you don't think I'm nice?"

And then we raced to the bathroom because we were laughing so hard, we risked wetting our skorts.

When I diagnosed myself with being too nice, Kate's reaction made me realize that perhaps I don't always see myself the way others see me. I have problems—who doesn't?—but apparently one of mine is not that I'm too nice. And even though I'm glad that I'm not such a desperate people pleaser anymore, I'd like to think I'm still a nice person. But what really makes a person nice? I decided to do a little research and set off for that citadel of knowledge—my bed, where I write books and scour the internet every day.

I googled "What makes a person nice?" and found many articles on what it means to be nice. My takeaway was that nice people are altruistic, honest, fair, generous, thoughtful, and kind. In other words, nice people are good people.

I know that many people believe they're good people, because when I was in college, I worked as a cashier at a busy Barnes & Noble bookstore in downtown Boston. It was a huge store, and people bought a lot of books back in the pre-tablet era. After I stepped behind the cash register at the beginning of my shift, there was almost never a lull.

After romance novels, the second most popular books people bought were in the self-help category—and there were a couple of blockbusters. Every shift I rang up copies of a book called *When Bad Things Happen to Good People*. I remember looking at the buyers of this book and thinking, *You can't all be good people*, and I was right, because people shoplifted from that store a lot, and when security caught them, this book was one of the more popular stolen items. Apparently, people who steal things believe they are good people who deserve good things to happen to them. Then they're gobsmacked when bad things happen, so they steal a book to try to sort it all out.

While scanning the web to unravel the mystery of what it means to be nice, I came across a 2011 study done at the University of Chicago that set out to determine if rats would perform acts of kindness with no reward or benefit to themselves. Rats who were trained to open the latches of cages, were allowed to roam freely in the study area, where other rats were contained in latched cages. The free rats routinely unlatched the cages and freed their friends. Perhaps the rat liberator just wanted companionship, one might conclude. But no. Somehow, the researchers were able to rig a setup in which the liberating rats would not be able to share space to fully reunite with the freed rat, yet they still unlatched the cages.

According to *The Guardian* newspaper, which reported on this study: "Even more astonishing, when the rats were presented with two cages, one containing a rat, the other chocolate, they chose to open both cages and they *typically shared the chocolate*." Italics are mine because, how cute is that? The researchers concluded that the rats were displaying empathy, an emotion that we humans like to think is ours alone and utterly devoid in other species. According to the head of this study, a researcher named Peggy Mason, there was nothing to motivate the rats "except whatever feeling they get from helping another individual."

Would I feel good freeing a caged person? Of course. Would I open the cage with the chocolate first, devour it, and then free the person? NO! I'd share. To be honest, though, I'd give the other person the entire chocolate because I don't really like chocolate. But this study made me ashamed of my hatred and fear of rats. I had no idea they were so kind and thoughtful. When I lived in Boston, an enormous rat ran across my sandaled foot outside a club one night and I can still feel its spongy little feet on my bare flesh; I can still hear my screams echoing off the buildings nearby as I fled. Now I realize I'd never taken the time to consider the rat's state of mind or motivation. That little fellow might have been rushing to help an elderly rat cross the street, or to enjoy a shared chocolate with a cherished friend.

The thing that most impressed me about the rat story wasn't just that rats can be altruistic—I've seen altruistic behavior in our many pets. I know that we aren't the only mammals who feel good helping others and have empathy for individuals who are suffering. What made the rats morally superior to some humans is that the rats didn't free the hostage rats to look good to the other rats. Their kindness wasn't performative. It was truly selfless. Humans are probably the only species who can be kind when others are looking, and less kind when nobody is watching. I'm thinking of a person I know who boasts about serving food to strangers at soup kitchens on Thanksgiving but is selfish and undermining to friends, family, and coworkers the rest of the time. I'm thinking of a writer/spirituality guru I know who is on a perpetual journey of truth and light on the written page but navigates the real world through a lens of seething envy and rage. I'm thinking, I guess, of me too, smiling gaily at Leslie, then savaging her behind her back.

Another woman I play tennis with—let's call her Beth—is the opposite extreme of Leslie. Beth, a retired schoolteacher, is a thoughtful, considerate, and honest tennis player. Unfortunately, she's not often available to play because she spends much of her time volunteering for hospice and teaching English as a second language to immigrants. Beth is a good person, but she's also a hardcore people pleaser and a serious self-doubter. The minute she arrives on the tennis court, she apologizes for being late. When told that she's actually a few minutes early, she apologizes for that. I find it hard not to over-apologize during a tennis game, but Beth takes it to the next level.

"I'm sorry!" Beth says every time she makes an error.

"Oh my gosh, I'm so sorry," she says when her partner makes an error.

When I'm her partner and tell her that it was my error, she says that she set me up poorly, it was really her fault. When her opponent hits a ball into the adjacent baseball field, Beth cries out, "I'm so sorry. I think . . . I think maybe it was out, but what do you think?" The idea that others might be unhappy for even a moment causes her visible pain. Even though it's nice that she's deeply empathetic, it hurts her game, and her apologies and constant self-recrimination begin to drain everybody's energy after a while.

Which brings me to Helen. Helen is about ten years older than me and is the type that everybody now describes as being "on the spectrum." I don't think an actual doctor would describe her that way, but everybody else does. I was first paired with Helen in a doubles match against another team a few years ago. We'd never met before, so I'd emailed her prior to the match to ask if she wanted to go to the park early so that we could warm up.

Her response: "No."

Not: "Oh my gosh, I'd love to, but I have to take my dog to the vet/pick up my kid/have a hysterectomy." Just no.

I soon learned that Helen is a very honest player. She doesn't blame others when she makes mistakes; she doesn't cheat or undermine. She also doesn't smile, high-five, tap rackets, or otherwise try to buoy the spirit of her partner. I learned this after she hit a beautiful winning serve. I gave her a big smile and when I went to tap her racket, she whipped it behind her as if I were trying to steal the thing. A little later, when we were down a few points, I said enthusiastically, "Don't worry, Helen, we've got this!"

"We're losing," she corrected me.

I tend to be a little over the top on the court (surprise!). I have a lot of nervous energy, I'm anxious about what my partner thinks of me, what the opponents think of me, what the people driving by think of me. I try to mask my anxiety by acting flippant and nonchalant. When I make blunders, I laugh and crack jokes, trying to stifle my inner mantra of: *I hate myself. I hate myself. I hate myself.*

So that day, I started off with my affable, goofball persona, but after a few stern "cut the crap" glances from Helen, I focused on the game. We ended up winning because I stopped trying to gauge everybody's happiness on the court and started mirroring Helen's no-nonsense attitude. Now Helen is my favorite partner. Helen isn't a barrel of laughs, but she's courteous. I've never heard her say an unkind thing about other players. On the other hand, I've never once heard her laugh.

The night after Kate laughed in my face when I told her I'm too nice, she called me, because she felt a little bad about it. We cackled again as we recalled it. But I said, "I really am nicer than most people, though, right?"

Kate was silent.

"Some people?"

Kate made a little squeaking noise that didn't sound like a yes.

"Leslie! I'm nicer than Leslie. Say it!" I demanded.

Kate complied with an adamant "Yes!" Then she told me that she wouldn't enjoy our friendship as much as she does if I were as nice as I seemed to think I was. "People who are too nice are boring," she said.

Maybe, but I'd still like to think of myself as somebody who is essentially kind. Or at least tries to be kind. Kindness is selfless, it doesn't come from a fear of rejection or a desire to be admired, it comes, in its purest form, from wanting, simply, to be good to others.

Last week, I was standing in the lobby of our gym/tennis club, chatting with some women I'd just played with. A much older woman approached in a stooped, shuffling fashion and instead of going around us, she growled, "Move!" and used her cane like a shepherd's staff to split our group in half so that she could walk straight ahead.

Somebody in the group said quietly, "Excuse us!" (somebody who was working on an essay about being nice).

Helen was with us. She said, "That's Eileen. She's ninety-six years old. She comes here every Tuesday for chair yoga."

"That's amazing," I said. "But if she can do yoga, she could walk a few extra steps and go around us."

Helen said, "She's ninety-six. How many minutes does she have left on this earth? How many more steps until she's stuck in the ground? She can't waste her time or energy being nice all the time."

And if I weren't afraid that she'd slap me, I would have hugged Helen, because a heavenly future revealed itself to me at that moment. I realized that if I'm lucky and watch my cholesterol, there will come a day when social angst and the desperation to please others will be my burden no more. Someday, when I'm much further along this increasingly dim, muffled path of life, I'll claim it as my own path, and I'll tell everybody else to move out of my damn way.

But I'll probably say please.

ACKNOWLEDGMENTS

I am so very grateful to my editor, publisher, and friend, Marysue Rucci, for her pitch-perfect editing and guidance. Many thanks to Emma Taussig, Jackie Seow, Patrick Sullivan, Hope Herr-Cardillo, Allison Har-zvi, Jessie McNeil, Ingrid Carabulea, Laura Jarrett, Clare Maurer, Carolyn Levin, and the rest of the Marysue Rucci team. Deepest appreciation as well to my wonderful literary agent, Margaret Riley King, who read early drafts of these essays and had great notes and inspiring words. Much gratitude as well to Meagan Irby, Sylvie Rabineau, and the rest of the WME team.

Several of these essays were previously published. I'd like to thank Ann Hood and W. W. Norton for including my essay "Needlers" in their anthology *Knitting Pearls: Writers Write about Knitting*. Thanks also to Leah Odze Epstein, Caren Osten, and Seal Press for including my essay, originally titled "The Slip," in their anthology *Drinking Diaries*. A slightly longer version appears in this collection under the title "Three-Drinks-Short." I'd also like to thank Lavinia Spalding for including my essay "The Godfather Town" in *The Best Women's Travel Writing, Volume 12,* as well as my friend Marcia DeSanctis for uniting us.

Much gratitude to Dan Jones, editor of the *New York Times*

Modern Love column, for publishing my essay "Rallying to Keep the Game Alive." A longer version appears in this collection under the title "Love Means Nothing (in Tennis)." Also to *Real Simple* magazine for publishing the essays that appear in this collection as "Empty Nest" and "Old Dog, New Tricks."

I wish to thank my dear friend Alice Hoffman, whose annual event, Pink Pages, has raised millions for breast cancer treatment at Mount Auburn Hospital in Cambridge, Massachusetts. I was thrilled Alice asked me to read at several of these literary galas, and a shorter version of the essay "My Life in Dogs" was written for Pink Pages.

Heartfelt love and gratitude to Laura Zigman for being such a wonderful friend, partner in (true) crime, reader, and confidante, and to the fabulous Julie Klam for the same.

I have too many other friends to thank here, but I'd like to express my love and appreciation to Martha Stewart and Charlotte Beers for their friendship and for being such wonderful examples of how to rock one's prime. I'm watching you two brilliant beauties and hope you will slow down to my pace one day. I'm also thankful to Dominique, Anni, Kate, Randy, Sebastian, Mike and Tracy—all of whom manage to make being nice look easy.

Who else, who else?

Oh! My mother and father, Meg and Paul, for letting me write about them and not minding the parts in these essays, and in life, where I tried to be nice but maybe could have tried harder.

As always, all my love and gratitude to my children, Jack and Devin.

And most of all, Denis.

ABOUT THE AUTHOR

Ann Leary is the *New York Times* bestselling author of the novels *The Foundling*, *The Children*, *The Good House*, *Outtakes from a Marriage*, and the memoir *An Innocent, a Broad*.

She has written for numerous publications including NPR, *Ploughshares*, *Real Simple*, and the *New York Times*. Her novel *The Good House* was adapted as a motion picture starring Sigourney Weaver and Kevin Kline.

Ann and her husband, Denis, live in New York.